WORK IT OUT!

What does it mean to follow Jesus?

ANTHONY DELANEY

anthonydelaney.com   **ivychurch**.org

Copyright © 2015
Second Edition 2018
All rights reserved

ISBN 978-0-9927271-3-0

Author: Anthony Delaney, Leader of Ivy Church
Editor and author of 'Word' chapter: Katie Levell
Executive Producer: Carl Brettle
Producer: Dave Hill
Design: Reeves Creative reevescreative.com
Illustration: Paul Marshall and Andy Smith

"*It all adds up! Finally, Anthony has managed to find a math that I can understand, which if you learn it, applies in the school of life.*"

Danielle Strickland (Infinitum)

"*This highly readable book can help clarify the purposes and trajectory of your life. Well worth a read...or two.*"

Alan Hirsch (100m)

"*A short but insightful read that can change lives forever – Anthony proves again that deep truths don't have to be complex.*"

Dave Ferguson (President - Exponential)

"*A great book, packed full of nuggets of wisdom and kernels of truth. Get it. Read it. Share it with others. More than anything, live it.*"

Malcolm Duncan (Spring Harvest)

"*Anthony is the real deal, a leader full of keen insights into how to unlock the gift and calling God has placed in you. Read this, then get hold of a bunch for your friends.*"

Carl Beech (CVM)

"*Simple, profound and greatly helpful. An absolute must read for anyone wanting to understand the basics of Christianity in a straightforward and powerful way.*"

Gavin Calver (Director of Mission - Evangelical Alliance)

CONTENTS

? QUESTIONS 6

❯ GREATER THAN 16

− SUBTRACT AND ÷ DIVIDE 30

✚ ADD 46

∞ INFINITY 62

✗ MULTIPLY 78

ADVANCE 94

WORD 98

? QUESTIONS

"Work out your salvation... for it is God who works in you."

Philippians 2:12-13

Maybe you've started thinking about whether there might be something more to life, or you've had some conversations with people which left you wondering about whether God is real. Or maybe there's been some significant stuff going on in your life, and you have started to consider what Christians actually believe. Whatever the reason you've picked up this book, you're very welcome.

WORK IT OUT is here to help you to work out the answers to some of your **?QUESTIONS** about God. This little book can be used as an individual study, but it's even better if you can **WORK IT OUT** in a reading group that meets every week, or why not form one online with friends? Like working out at the gym, it's good to be committed if you want to get anything out of it, and sometimes that's easier to do with others. But even when you go it alone, you're not really on your own — this is a joint venture. As you invest some time and energy, you will find that God has already given everything you need to find your way back to him. When you let him in, you will notice how he works in you. As you start working it out with him, you'll see the work he's doing through you.

Do you remember your first day at school? I remember my first day at High School. It was freezing and I had my parka zipped up all the way, which helped hide my fears and my face. I got to the bike sheds and two massive lads were fighting. I was in a strange new world.

I tried my best not to talk to anyone until lunchtime. My mate Dave and I stood and did a little dance on the benches in the playground, just for a laugh, which ended up with us getting 'six of the best' from the woodwork teacher who made them. That was how education worked back then.

I even remember starting Primary School. Mum said I was grown up enough for school now, and I believed her of course, because you believe your Mum. I was four. I was hungry for knowledge — even though I knew a lot of things already.

I knew the alphabet.

I knew I needed a best friend at school.

I knew girls were soppy.

I knew that when I tied my duffle coat arms around my neck like a cape, I could fly: it was just a matter of time....

Then the reality of life hit hard.

I found that I still had a lot to learn.

Morgan Evans knocked down my brick tower in the morning. John Gialluca pinched my Kit Kat from my lunchbox at lunchtime. At playtime one of the boys got himself in some trouble in the urinals, thinking that was where you sat and waited to use the real toilets. By the end of week one, I had let a girl who wanted to be a hairdresser when she grew up cut my hair with the paper scissors.

I had big **? QUESTIONS**. Why did Mr Fleming the caretaker carry around a big bucket of sawdust? I found out the answer to that when the school dinners were brought out... and brought back up.

Whether we're still in school or not, teachers or pupils, we all still have a lot to learn about life. In fact, it's probably true that the longer we live, the bigger the **? QUESTIONS** we have.

So where do we go to get answers?

In this book we're going to be looking at some of those great big **? QUESTIONS** everybody has. You're not the first to ask them. Many of life's greatest **? QUESTIONS** were posed to, by and about Jesus Christ, in response to his life, death, resurrection and teaching.

Be prepared to discover that Jesus answered people's **? QUESTIONS** not necessarily how they wanted to be answered, but with what they needed to hear. As if there really were not just opinions.... but answers. And he had the authority to give them.

One of the people who had a few **? QUESTIONS** to ask Jesus was someone who was probably meant to have all the answers. His name was Nicodemus, and he was a wise man and statesman in the Jewish nation. But he came on the quiet to Jesus late one night with his biggest life **?QUESTIONS**. He wanted to get Jesus' take on them.

I think that was a smart move. Maybe he came at night because he was in the dark about some things to do with God and how people relate to him. I love and admire that this clever and influential guy still realised he had a lot to learn and was humble enough to come and ask.

You might consider yourself pretty clued up about Christianity, or this might all be new to you. Maybe you are checking out this God stuff on the quiet too. You're in good company.

You may not be particularly religious but Nicodemus was a strict Pharisee: one of the leading religious people of the day. In his eyes Jesus was probably nothing more than a travelling teacher — a Rabbi — with some interesting views and surrounded by startling rumours about miracles he was supposed to be doing.

Nicodemus had obviously seen or heard of something special going on with this Jesus character — that he came up with accurate answers, and asked great **?QUESTIONS** that provoked people to find their own answers.

He knew that Jesus had a unique kind of authority somehow, in everything he said and did.

Let's look at what Jesus' friend John said happened when they met that night.

How's your Bible navigation?
If it's all new to you, take a look at the Word chapter at the back of this book — it'll point you in the right direction.

Now there was a Pharisee, a man named Nicodemus who was a member of the Jewish ruling council. He came to Jesus at night and said, "Rabbi, we know that you are a teacher who has come from God. For no one could perform the signs you are doing if God were not with him."

Jesus replied, "Very truly I tell you, no one can see the kingdom of God unless they are born again."

"How can someone be born when they are old?" Nicodemus asked. "Surely they cannot enter a second time into their mother's womb to be born!"

Jesus answered, "Very truly I tell you, no one can enter the kingdom of God unless they are born of water and the Spirit. Flesh gives birth to flesh, but the Spirit gives birth to spirit. You should not be surprised at my saying, 'You must be born again.' The wind blows wherever it pleases. You hear its sound, but you cannot tell where it comes from or where it is going. So it is with everyone born of the Spirit."

"How can this be?" Nicodemus asked.

"You are Israel's teacher," said Jesus, "and do you not understand these things?"

John 3:1-10 (NIV)

The conversation kicked off cordially enough on Nicodemus' side with him basically complimenting Jesus on being a great teacher. But Jesus launched straight in with, "You need to get your eyes tested to see what God wants you to see. You need to get your heart checked. You're supposed to be the *teacher*. But you need to go back to your school days. You need to become a child again!"

Not child-ish. Childlike.

Why? To get the lesson Jesus wanted to teach.

Then Jesus coined a phrase that has since taken on all kinds of weird connotations. He said, "You must be born, again."

He wasn't recommending a one-off God-lesson, he was describing a completely new life.

He didn't mean a physical birth, he meant a spiritual birth. Jesus was saying to Nicodemus, "If you're ever going to live like God's child, it starts all over again, with a revolution from the inside out."

New life starts the way the old one did. You must be born again.

> **SOMEONE ASKS, "CAN YOU SEE GOD? I'VE NEVER SEEN GOD!"**
>
> **"WELL, I'VE NEVER SEEN THE WIND – I'VE SEEN THE EFFECT OF THE WIND. AND I'VE NEVER SEEN GOD, BUT I'VE SEEN THE EFFECT OF GOD!"**
>
> Billy Graham

Jesus told Nicodemus you can't predict what God will do any more than you can predict the wind. You might have more degrees than a thermometer, but don't kid yourself. You can't understand all about how God works any more than you can understand how the wind blows.

The wind is air in motion. It blows people's umbrellas inside out, makes pollination possible and carries tomorrow's weather in. We can measure its, speed and direction, but we can't control it. As anyone who has ever believed the weatherman knows, it's just not that predictable.

Jesus wants us at the humble starting point that says you can't ever fully figure out God and how he works. He advised Nicodemus, "Don't try to use your cleverness or your power to work it out. God is found when you start your spiritual life, when you connect to Him inside — you become a new person." So the first thing you need to know about God is that you can't know everything about him. He's bigger than our boxes.

Now Nicodemus was having some trouble getting to grips with this, but Jesus carried on: "You haven't even got a clue who I really am."

Wow! Right between the eyes!

"I THINK IT'S A DEFINING QUESTION FOR A CHRISTIAN: WHO WAS CHRIST? AND I DON'T THINK YOU'RE LET OFF EASILY BY SAYING 'A GREAT THINKER' OR 'A GREAT PHILOSOPHER,' BECAUSE ACTUALLY, HE WENT ROUND SAYING HE WAS THE MESSIAH. THAT'S WHY HE WAS CRUCIFIED: HE WAS CRUCIFIED BECAUSE HE SAID HE WAS THE SON OF GOD. SO, EITHER HE, IN MY VIEW, WAS THE SON OF GOD, OR HE WAS NUTS. FORGET ROCK AND ROLL MESSIANIC COMPLEXES, THIS IS LIKE CHARLIE MANSON-TYPE DELIRIUM.

"AND I FIND IT HARD TO ACCEPT THAT ALL THE MILLIONS AND MILLIONS OF LIVES, HALF THE EARTH FOR TWO THOUSAND YEARS, HAVE BEEN TOUCHED, FELT THEIR LIVES TOUCHED AND INSPIRED, BY SOME NUTTER. I JUST DON'T BELIEVE IT."

Bono

He was making a point about the way Nicodemus had addressed him — "Good teacher."

If you were to read the whole of John's account of Jesus' life, you'd find its whole point is to demonstrate and help you believe that Jesus really is the Son of God. He's not just another good teacher or moral philosopher from the world's history, but its Saviour from eternity.

That's what Nicodemus had to see first, before he could see anything of what God's kingdom was really about. Jesus was not and is not just 'a good teacher.'

Why don't you take a look at **John 1:1-18**, which has all these wonderful titles of who Jesus really is, from what John saw and worked out in all his eye-witness moments.

First he's called the **WORD OF GOD**, who was there in the beginning, the creative force of the whole universe, come to spell out the **LOVE OF GOD** in ways and language we can understand. Jesus is also the **LIGHT OF THE WORLD** — for all people — so they don't have to stumble in darkness any more. John then goes on to call him the **CHRIST**, which means the one who was anointed: chosen to do a particular job, selected for the role. He's the **LAMB OF GOD** — that's about sacrifice and paying the debt of each and every person. He's also called the **KING OF ISRAEL** to show that he was born into the family line of God's special people, to bring a totally new concept of royalty to that nation. He is the **SON OF MAN**, human, actually born as a baby, knowing what it's like to live on this earth. But above all Jesus is the **SON OF GOD** who is completely powerful and completely perfect: the only one who could save the world.

And hidden in this short section right at the beginning of the story of Jesus' human life on Earth is the formula for the **?QUESTIONS** that Nicodemus was asking. The deepest and most profound miracle, but wrapped up in a little sum which is not hard to work out at all. Even a child could do it....

> *...to all who did* **RECEIVE** *him, to those who* **BELIEVED** *in his name, he gave the right to* **BECOME** *children of God...*
> John 1:12 (NIV)

RECEIVE ✚ BELIEVE = BECOME

In fact, maybe a child finds it easier to work out than an adult.

God gave us on the Earth a present, the gift of his own Son, so that we could know him, God, personally.

Kids love gifts. They don't have any problem with them: they plan their birthday parties for months in advance and write enormous long letters to Santa. They aren't even that interested in the basics — where the next meal is coming from or how the rent is paid — as long as they can rely on someone else to do that for them.

Jesus wanted Nicodemus to understand that you have to be born again, to start again, so that you can be dependent again, like a child. Depending on God, not yourself.

Another time, Jesus said,

> *"...if you sinful people know how to give good gifts to your children, how much more will your heavenly Father give good gifts to those who ask him?"*
>
> Matthew 7:11 (NLT)

What do you need to **RECEIVE** from God? He loves to provide, like any good dad. Going back to our sum from before, if you're going to get the answers you're looking for, you need to accept that first and most important gift, the one John spoke about — Jesus — into your life.

The next part of the sum is the one about **BELIEVING**. It's so much harder for an adult, but children do it all the time. **BELIEVING**. They **BELIEVE** their parents love them. They **BELIEVE** that their mum will be there at the school gates to pick them up like she said she would. They **BELIEVE** that there is gold at the end of the rainbow and that the little boy who just started school really can fly when he wears his duffle coat cape around his neck.

They just trust, even though some things don't prove to be reliable. When we're grown up we call it being gullible, and if you can't truly trust someone then it probably is. But when you're talking about God...? Can you trust God? Do you **BELIEVE** that he is who he says he is? Do you dare to?

I want to invite you to **BELIEVE** that he **LOVES** you, that he **ACCEPTS** you just the way you are, that he can **TAKE CARE OF YOUR NEEDS**, be your **COMFORT** and your **GUIDE**.

Can you **BELIEVE** it? Because that's the answer. Becoming like a child again so that we can **RECEIVE** and **BELIEVE** all that God says to us. It's not about making it happen, studying until it all makes sense. It is about going back to the most basic truth there is, and starting a whole new life.

If you **RECEIVE** what God provides, and **BELIEVE** what God promises, you'll gain a position you could never achieve by yourself: you'll **BECOME** a child of God. In his family, forever....

WORK OUT

Everyone has **?QUESTIONS**. You won't always be able to **WORK IT OUT** on your own. But there are others who have been living out this **RECEIVING** and **BELIEVING** formula for a good while now, and they might well have some of the answers.

If you know some Christians nearby, get in touch with them. They would love to invite you to their church. No pressure.

If you don't, we should be able to help. Go online to **alpha.org/try** and find your location on the map.

Or if you're ever passing Manchester, why not call in and meet me at Ivy Church for one of our services. All the information and lots of free resources are here: **ivychurch.org**

CONNECT

Thank you God for sending Jesus, your Son. I may not understand it all yet but I really want to get to know you.

Please help me to trust you, so that I can start a new life again, learning how to be your child.

› GREATER THAN

"Everything is possible for one who believes."
Mark 9:23 (NIV)

Time *Magazine* ran a startling cover story recently: CAN *GOOGLE SOLVE DEATH?*

The article details how the clever people behind the world's biggest search engine are now searching for a way to help people live forever.

Interesting, hey? I'm not sure I'd *actually* want to live forever if the world just stays like this, but death is the one human problem that eventually everyone will have to face, and the Bible would say it has in fact already been solved.

Not by Google.

Not by people searching.

But by God coming to search for us. By God coming to find and save people. Jesus came to show us what God is really like, then he died and rose from the dead so we could not only know about him, but really know him.

Death is a scary thing. It's a great power. The Bible calls it 'The Last Enemy.' But it's a defeated enemy. Because God is greater. Greater than anything. Greater than death.

We're going to return to that little formula for becoming God's children that we looked at in **? QUESTIONS**. We'll work on it and expand it out and put ourselves into it — even introducing some more maths symbols to **WORK IT OUT**.

Just because you **BELIEVE**, doesn't mean you don't have questions. You probably have a lot more!

As we saw in the previous chapter, we all have big questions in our lives, and it would be nice if I could say to you, "Well, if you look in the Bible, that will give you the answer."

Really? I open up the Bible and see a snake striking up a conversation... seas parting... crazy plagues... fire from heaven... is that a talking donkey? Very, very old people — having babies... water flowing out of a rock... walking on water... water being turned into wine?

Really?

How do we explain these things? I've read the Bible through cover to cover countless times but there are still times I'm reading it and going, "Woah! Isn't that a bit unlikely? In fact — isn't that impossible? How can that happen?"

> **SCIENCE IS POWERLESS TO ANSWER QUESTIONS SUCH AS "WHY DID THIS UNIVERSE COME INTO BEING?" "WHAT IS THE MEANING OF HUMAN EXISTENCE?" AND "WHAT HAPPENS AFTER WE DIE?"**
>
> Francis Collins, head of the Human Genome Project, *The Language of God*

Suddenly the know-all atheist at the Rose and Crown seems to have a point when he says that "Surely science has disproved religion... and just how did Noah get all those animals into the ark?"

Now, part of the answer is that science and religion are often asking very different questions, which is why they seem sometimes to be at odds with one another. Science can answer some of the **HOW?** but it's not great at telling us the **WHY?**

The tough truth is, you can't get away with saying these supernatural events are all just stories to teach us a lesson or help us to think in a new way, because most of them are not presented as pictures and metaphors. The Bible says these things actually happened.

In history.

Miracles that went against what we call 'the laws of nature.'

Because somebody prayed, it didn't rain for years, then he prayed again and it poured down. Because somebody prayed, a blind man saw, a lame man walked.

It says various prophets, and Jesus, and his followers really healed people from illnesses. It says thousands of people were supernaturally fed from hardly any raw materials — not just once but a few times.

How do these impossible things happen? How does the impossible become possible?

Can God heal? Or speak? Or inspire the writers of a book so that it becomes his word to us?

Mary having a baby — Jesus — when she was still a virgin seems to be a sticking point for many. How can *that* happen?

The answer is in this symbol:

❯ GREATER THAN

It means, what you put on the left of the symbol is greater than whatever you put on the right.

Is your God ❯ **GREATER THAN** your problem? Is the God you picture ❯ **GREATER THAN** impossibility? Mine is!

That virgin birth, for example. It is impossible! It's not presented as normal in the Bible. And that's the point. It had never happened before the angel turned up to Mary and announced that a child who was the Son of God was to be born in that special way and that she was to call him Jesus.

Mary had understandable questions about this happening — not least because she was the virgin who was going to be involved!

But she asked, "How can this be?" Not, "This can't be!" That's what having an open mind really looks like. Have you got an open mind?

God doesn't mind us having questions, and the answer she got blew her mind and invited her trust.

"The Holy Spirit will do it, the power of God will do it, because NOTHING is impossible with God."

You can read the whole conversation for yourself in **Luke 1:26-37.**

The angel was asking, "Mary, do you believe God is ❯ **GREATER THAN?**"

God is ❯ **GREATER THAN** the impossible!

Nothing is impossible for God. He's always doing something! The only thing that is not possible, if God's Holy Spirit power is operating, is that nothing would happen.

Mary said, **"May it be to me as you have said."** She **BELIEVED** what she was told and instead of voicing doubt she spoke that **BELIEF** out and

RECEIVED what she had been promised.

She **BELIEVED** what God said, and she **RECEIVED** what God promised. Because nothing is impossible.

When her God-child Jesus grew up and started his ministry, that became one of his most common recurring messages, in what he said and what he did. It says all kinds of people were brought to him with all kinds of diseases and he healed them all.

How?

This is how Jesus described it:

> *"With man, this is impossible, but with God all things are possible."*
> Matthew 19:26 (NIV)

We think it can't happen. God thinks differently! All kinds of things are possible, if you put that kind of God in the equation. God is **❯ GREATER THAN**.

Jesus went even further though, and said that if we **BELIEVE** — that is, you and I — then nothing will be impossible for us!

Because our God is **❯ GREATER THAN**. He's **❯ GREATER THAN** anything in life and even **❯ GREATER THAN** death.

Jesus showed that 2000 years ago on the first ever Easter morning, when several women went to his tomb, fully expecting him to be there, dead. Instead they found an angel, who told them that he'd gone. Got up, and walked out. And that soon they'd see him face to face.

> *"Do not be afraid, for I know that you are looking for Jesus, who was crucified. He is not here; he has risen, just as he said. Come and see the place where he lay. Then go quickly and tell his disciples: 'He has risen from the dead and is going ahead of you into Galilee. There you will see him'."*
>
> Matthew 28:5-7 (NIV)

Later in the Bible we meet a man called Paul, who had the most amazing experience that completely turned his life around. You can read about it in

Acts 9:1-18. From that point onwards, he dedicated his life to explaining to people about who Jesus was, and what that meant for their lives.

He wrote letters to all the people who he'd helped to **BELIEVE** in and **RECEIVE** Jesus, and in one of these, there is a paragraph where he talks about Jesus beating death:

> *"...[Jesus] died for our sins, exactly as Scripture tells it; that he was buried; that he was raised from death on the third day, again exactly as Scripture says; that he presented himself alive to Peter, then to his closest followers, and later to more than five hundred of his followers all at the same time, most of them still around (although a few have since died); that he then spent time with James and the rest of those he commissioned to represent him; and that he finally presented himself alive to me."*

1 Corinthians 15:3-8 (MSG)

Jesus died, was buried, and in three days — surprise! — he was popping in unexpectedly on the same people who saw him die on a cross. Then he carried on making appearances to people, including his own brother James (who hadn't believed that he really was who he said he was — all those names and titles that we looked at in the last chapter — until he saw him physically come alive again).

And Paul admits, "Me too! I was anti-Jesus! I thought he was a dead false prophet and his followers were starting up a deluded cult. Then I went from chief enemy to chief supporter when — surprise! — he appeared and told me how wrong I was."

Now, just to confirm, these aren't the same kind of appearances people claim to experience on the news sometimes. You pick up the paper and read about someone saying, "I saw Jesus' face on my piece of toast."

When Paul said that Jesus 'appeared' and people 'saw him,' he means exactly that — they saw him in the flesh. Jesus wasn't an apparition; he was alive!

"Touch me and see — I'm real!"

I've visited Jerusalem where you can visit the Tomb of the Holy Sepulchre. It's advertised as the place where Jesus' body lay, and when you go there it's a grand building, highly decorated and made to look impressive. But of course we don't know actually where Jesus' body lay. The first Christians didn't need to make a shrine or worship at the tomb... because he isn't there!

Jesus is alive!

The bones of Mohammed are in Medina. The bones of Buddha are divided up and worshipped in various countries.

But Christians worship Jesus because his tomb was empty: we make no bones about it!

After being killed brutally, his physical body — not some ghost — was raised back to life physically. Alone of all the world's great religious figures, he's alive forevermore.

> **YOU'RE AT A CROSSROADS, LOOKING FOR DIRECTIONS, AND TWO MEN ARE THERE. ONE'S DEAD, ONE'S ALIVE. WHICH ONE ARE YOU GOING TO ASK?!**
>
> J. John

Those people touched him, talked to him, ate meals with him, hugged him. He appeared to people alone, and in pairs, and to hundreds. In person — face-to-face. They believed in him. But even so (and we can see that the Bible's the most honest book in the world because it doesn't shy away from this) right up to the very end, Gospel writer Matthew says, **"...but some doubted"** 28:17 (NIV).

The same things can happen to two people, and one could find a supernatural explanation for it and the other might say, "No, it's an illusion." Because that's what they believe. They believe the supernatural can't happen. So if something happens that looks to be supernatural, there has to be another explanation.

Some believed, and some doubted, but the resurrection of Jesus Christ is a matter of **FAITH** and **FACT**. Facts you can check out, that lead to faith in someone you can trust. This isn't about proof.

"Well, prove to me that God exists and I'll believe."

From my experience as a police officer I can tell you, you don't look for proof, you look for good evidence. Then you lay that evidence out for people to decide for themselves what they believe it proves.

In the passage we just looked at from 1 Corinthians, Paul described that evidence for Jesus coming back to life — the resurrection. He said it's of first importance. The greatest event in history — not just a little bit important, like who won the cup or who lost the battle — it's the greatest day in history! Why? Because if people saw Jesus face-to-face, if Jesus really did die and then rise again, then two things are true:

First, **YOU CAN KNOW GOD**.

I don't presume to know what you think of Jesus yet. Looking at his teachings you might think he was a wise prophet who spoke for God. Looking at his healings, you might think he was a humanitarian who worked for God. Looking at the cross you might say he was a revolutionary and a martyr who died for God.

But as we saw in the last chapter, Jesus didn't say he was just a teacher, a prophet or a healer, a martyr for the cause. He said he was the Son of God, and when people called him that he never corrected them but encouraged them. The resurrection changes everything. It meant that Jesus is who he claimed to be. Jesus can do what he said he can do. It proves that Jesus is God. And you'll notice I don't refer to Jesus in the past tense — because he is still alive. While you're reading this, he's reading you!

So you can know him. Now. He is really God, and God is real, and God is knowable.

Second, the fact that people saw Jesus after he'd died and come alive again means that **ALL THINGS ARE POSSIBLE**. Miracles are possible. If God could raise Jesus from the grave, what can't happen? Put anything alongside that new possibility and suddenly impossible no longer applies.

New life is possible. Jesus said, *"I have come that you may have life and have it to the full" John 10:10* (NIV). And the resurrection says it's available.

New life. New for old. Freedom and forgiveness. For you.

God is knowable and all things are possible, because Jesus' life is **> GREATER THAN** death's power.

There's a phrase that people say, "If you believe that, you'll believe anything." They say it as if it's a bad thing.

But you can believe that Jesus is alive. Look at the evidence from the Bible, from history, from the lives being changed right now because of him, all around the world. It's true! It really happened.

If you believe that, you can believe anything!

If God can do that, he can do anything!

And he did it!

People sometimes talk about faith as wishful thinking or blind belief, like faith is some kind of mental drug or positive thinking that helps you hang on in there when times are tough.

For me, faith is a confident belief in who Jesus is and what he has done. The Bible says Jesus is the same yesterday, today and forever, so I know because of yesterday that nothing is impossible, today or tomorrow.

Whatever happens and whatever we face, God is always **> GREATER THAN**.

I've had people say to me, "I wish I had faith like you."

Sometimes I discover what they really mean is a kind of patronising, "I could never be as gullible as you."

But the truth is they can have faith: you can have faith. As a famous sportswear brand says, "Impossible is Nothing!" You just have to trust that God is **> GREATER THAN**. He's greater than impossible.

> [God] is able to do immeasurably more than we can ask or imagine....
> Ephesians 3:20 (NIV)

Does that encourage you?

We're not just blindly wishing for things, we can actually talk to God about achieving the impossible. He wants to hear our dreams and our ambitions for wonderful things, so the world he loves can be put back the way he wants it, starting with you and me.

This is what prayer is. Connecting to a God who is **❯ GREATER THAN** means knowing that you are asking someone who is more powerful than the problem. Because then faith in God is not blind faith, wishful thinking, it's the most sensible and obvious response.

Sometimes people suggest that miracles can't happen because of the laws of nature. Check the dictionary though: here's what supernatural means: **❯ GREATER THAN** nature.

Who made nature? Who makes the laws? I don't have enough faith to believe that nature just made itself. God made the universe. God is **❯ GREATER THAN** the universe he made and stands outside of it, but he can and does choose to enter it.

> **WHAT IS NATURE ANYWAY? IT IS BUT THE CREATION OF GOD, THE MAKER OF ALL THINGS. AND WHAT ARE THE LAWS OF NATURE BUT THE LAWS OF GOD, THROUGH WHICH HE GOVERNS THE MATERIAL WORLD. PRAYER DOES NOT VIOLATE ANY NATURAL LAW. GOD MAY SET ASIDE ONE LAW FOR THE HIGHER WORKING OF ANOTHER LAW, AND THIS HE MAY DO WHEN HE ANSWERS PRAYER. OR, GOD MAY ANSWER PRAYER BY WORKING THROUGH THE COURSE OF NATURAL LAW... WHETHER WE UNDERSTAND IT OR NOT.**
>
> EM Bounds *The Weapon of Prayer*

As scientists study the universe with all the forming and exploding stars, the black holes, the movements of light and matter, with new theories put forward and disproved, new laws discovered and revealed, we have come to realise that the rules we think are rules could be totally different in space and time. We find out more, we realise that all of creation is not as simple as we once thought. But God, the eternal, powerful God, makes the rules. And the God who makes the rules also makes the miracles.

Put a God that big on the left-hand side of the **❯ GREATER THAN** symbol, and frankly I don't care what you put on the right-hand side.

If he decides to do something, he can.

Think about it. The story we read in the Bible about Jesus walking on the water: you can check it out in **Matthew 14:22-33.**

How did Jesus walk on water? Was it a trick like when Dynamo walked on the Thames? Was it an optical illusion? Done with mirrors?

No - his integrity would not line up with such trickery.

What about the law of gravity?

Jesus is **❭ GREATER THAN** the law of gravity. God made gravity.

We are all subject to the law of gravity. If you let go of a heavy object, it will fall. The law of gravity says that planes can't fly. But a **❭ GREATER THAN**, the law of aerodynamics, overrides that. When the thrust of the engine is greater than the wind drag, the plane moves forward. And when the plane's speed is fast enough, the up lift of air under the wings becomes greater than the pull downwards of the weight of the plane: the plane takes off. I know it's true because I've been on a plane. For a long time flight was just a theory, but then the Wright brothers took off, and from then on it's not just a theory, it's fact!

You have your own questions, too. Put a **❭ GREATER THAN** God into the equation and you have to change impossible to possible. You change hopelessness to hope. All things are possible with God.

You might think with that amazing truth to activate us, people who go to church and call themselves Christians would be seeing miracles happen all over the place! How powerful is God?!

But the fact is, we don't often live like this. A guy called J B Phillips even wrote a book about it, called *Your God is Too Small.* He was saying that people don't see the possibilities, only the drawbacks. Putting God in a box, as though he has limits. We draw the symbol the other way: our God, our faith, is **❬ LESS THAN**. Do you think that affects the outcome? Do you think we see a different result in our lives and our prayers? What is the point of praying to someone who is **❬ LESS THAN** able to do anything?

We can settle for a **❬ LESS THAN** than Jesus wanted for us: he wants to break out of the boxes we put him in.

It's not God's plan for us to be living with a sense of failure and **❰ LESS THAN** .

In fact, his plan was the exact opposite. We can't even imagine what is possible. Take that sentence from Paul's letter to the Ephesians which you might have spotted earlier:

> *"[God] is able to do immeasurably more than all we ask or imagine...."*

I didn't actually put in the final part of that sentence, but this is where it gets personal:

> *"...according to his power that is at work within us."*
> Ephesians 3:20 (NIV)

Within us!

He is completely powerful and has unimaginable plans... to complete through us!

Jesus also said it:

> *"The person who trusts me will not only do what I'm doing but even greater things, because I, on my way to the Father, am giving you the same work to do that I've been doing. You can count on it. From now on, whatever you request along the lines of who I am and what I am doing, I'll do it. That's how the Father will be seen for who he is in the Son. I mean it. Whatever you request in this way, I'll do."*
>
> John 14:12-14 (MSG)

I don't exactly know what that means. I can understand that Jesus would say we get to do the same kind of miracles that he did when he was on the Earth. That we would pray for the sick and see them get better, see people getting released from debt and poverty and trapped lives set free. But greater than?

❱ GREATER THAN?

Greater miracles than Jesus did? Greater events than the dead rising? Greater in power than The Last Enemy? What does **❱ GREATER THAN** mean here? To you? Wouldn't you like to find out?

How would your life change if you dared to believe that "with God, all things are possible?" Start today!

WORKOUT

Think of a thing that seems impossible — something that you think Jesus would love to change. It might be someone who is sick, or a bad debt, or a difficult work relationship. Or something positive but it just seems not possible, like a new job or a relationship. Write it down. Start to tell God about it, **CONNECT** with the one who is ❯ *GREATER THAN* and ask him to make your impossible possible.

_____

_____

_____

_____

_____

_____

_____

_____

_____

_____

CONNECT

Jesus, powerful God, you are ❯ *GREATER THAN* my doubts and fears and problems. You're ❯ *GREATER THAN* sickness. You make the rules and you make the miracles and you are King over all the Earth. I believe that you have greater things for me in this life, and that with you all things are possible. Help me to live like that.

➖ SUBTRACT AND ➗ DIVIDE

"Whoever wants to be my disciple must deny themselves and take up their cross and follow me."

Mark 8:34 (NIV)

When I first met Zoe Delaney (who was not then Zoe Delaney, but is now my wife) she was a Christian and I was not. If you'd asked me I would have said that I was "some sort of Christian." Why? Because I was brought up in a 'Christian country' and I had some religious and church input through school... none of which I actually believed.

At times I'd even try to argue with her that I was "just as good a Christian as anyone else." The annoying thing was, she didn't argue back. But one day she gave me a Bible. I still have it. I thought it was a funny kind of gift to give someone. She watched me open it.

Inside the front cover she'd written,

"To Anthony, Mark 8.34, Love Zoe."

Love!

"Love Zoe," hey?! Hmmmm....

I thought I was on to a winner. Now I just had to crack the code. What did Mark 8:34 mean?

I knew she'd been out with a guy called Mark previously. Maybe this was saying she liked me better than him?

But then she told me how to work out how to find things in the Bible, and so I turned to Mark's report of Jesus' life: chapter 8 and verse 34. There was the sentence, and she'd helpfully underlined it for me. I read it out loud:

> *'Then he called the crowd to him along with his disciples and said: "Whoever wants to be my disciple must deny themselves and take up their cross and follow me".' (NIV)*

Deny myself?

Take up my cross?

I said to her, "I don't know what this means."

And she replied, "The fact that you don't know what it means shows you're not a Christian."

She was right. It was only when I became a Christian, a follower, disciple of Jesus Christ, that I realised that the joy, comfort and hope we have from God comes because we need it. We need it because of the pain, discouragement and frustration that being a disciple inevitably brings.

There needs to be a cross, a death, before the new life can happen, and it reappears at plenty of stages along the way as we 'work out our salvation.'

"I'M THINKING OF BECOMING A CHRISTIAN BECAUSE I'VE HEARD IT ADDS SOME THINGS ONTO MY LIFE."

That death happens when you stop living for yourself, and start your new, born-again life with Jesus. But we're not living a perfect heavenly life yet, and while we're still on the Earth, death and all its threats will continue to attack from time to time.

Of course, being a Christian transforms life so much that without Jesus it's impossible for us to live life to the full. We are going to look at that in the next few chapters.

But we can have a tendency to skip straight to the addition — what will this add to me? If you're only in this for what you get out of it, you will soon get out of it.

Christians have been guilty of just talking about what Jesus adds to your life. Say a quick prayer in a church meeting, put your hand up and from then on, you're a winner! Walking on the victory side, having your 'best life now.' No struggles, suffering, sin to deal with.

But Jesus didn't do that. If we read what he said in the biographies others wrote about him, it becomes painfully clear that before getting to ✚ **ADDITION**, we have to face the fact that there will be ➖ **SUBTRACTION** at times.

➖ SUBTRACT

The truth is, Jesus said that following him would make you a loser. Take up your cross....

> **YOU ONLY BECOME AN OVERCOMER BY GOING THROUGH WHAT YOU HAVE TO UNDERGO.**

We follow a man who was sent to a cross and died. Everyone in the time of Roman rule knew that someone carrying a cross was marked out as the ultimate loser. You would have to carry it through the streets so that everyone you passed could spit at, scorn or at best pity you as your defeat was shamefully paraded and publicly celebrated.

A warning. To everyone. 'Here, this, is a loser — Caesar always wins.'

> **"OH NO, IF YOU'RE LOOKING FOR SOMETHING TO ADD TO YOUR LIFE, BUDDHISM IS WAY COOLER AND ALL THAT MEDITATION HAS TO DE-STRESS YOU AND GIVE YOU PEACE OF MIND."**

Historians say that you would most likely not carry the whole thing, just the cross bar, called the *patibulum*, which they'd nail you to, then lift you up onto a verticle pole in a rubbish dump to wait in excruciating pain for death.

As Jesus was struggling along the Via Dolorosa in Jerusalem, onlookers would have seen a loser. A man carrying a massive ➖ **SUBTRACTION** sign, to an appointment with certain death.

Just a few weeks earlier, he had been talking to his disciples about exactly this subject. Matthew records him saying,

> *"Whoever does not take up his cross and follow me is not worthy of me. Whoever finds his life will"* *what!?* *"lose it, and whoever loses his life for my sake will find it."*

> Matthew 10:38-39 (NIV)

What did he mean by that?

We're going to look at the situation where he said that in a moment, and you could read the whole of Chapter 10 of Matthew's account yourself. But what does it mean to you, that if you really want to be his follower, his disciple, you are going to have to take up your cross too?

It means you become a loser. Because taking up your cross is ➡ **SUBTRACTION**. It's denying yourself. And the world would never say winners do that, so it looks to all the world like you joined the losing side.

For over 2000 years now, many of Jesus' disciples have known what losing for his sake really looks like.

Even before Jesus died on the cross and became alive again, before he'd witnessed those amazing events, Jesus' friend and follower Peter exclaimed to Jesus, **"We have left everything to follow you!" Matthew 19:27 (NIV)** And they had: job, family, home.

But that was only the beginning. This was before Peter was himself beaten up and imprisoned for daring to believe and sharing the truth about Jesus. Before, as historians believe, he was eventually killed by being hung upside down on a cross.

Then there was Paul, who also chose to live for Jesus and not for his own safety. He was imprisoned many times, often beaten to within an inch of his life, taking a total of 195 lashes with the whip, three beatings with rods and was pelted with stones and left for dead. All for what he described as 'my good news.'

Good news?! It doesn't sound like good news.

> But whatever were gains to me I now consider loss for the sake of Christ. What is more, I consider everything a loss because of the surpassing worth of knowing Christ Jesus my Lord, for whose sake I have lost all things. I consider them garbage...
>
> Philippians 3:7-8 (NIV)

How did they manage to go through all that? Paul once explained it using accounts terminology — profit and loss — to show how he viewed these events. He listed all the things that he had once viewed as profit: his privileged background, his high place in religious society, his good deeds: everything, bad or good, and compared it to knowing Jesus. He took a long look at this life list, and every single thing that he had once put in the profit column, he now wrote over with the word **LOSS**!

He'd rather lose anything, than lose the one who'd found and saved him.

And believers after Peter and Paul from the earliest times up until today have suffered loss, ➡ **SUBTRACTION**. Subtraction wasn't exceptional for the early Christians. It was expected. That you would lose your life to follow Jesus.

Here's how Paul describes it:

> *"I have been crucified with Christ and I no longer live, but Christ lives in me. The life I now live in the body, I live by faith in the Son of God, who loved me and gave himself for me."*
>
> Galatians 2:20 (NIV)

When you become a Christ-follower you lose your old way of life, lose your old bad habits and behaviours, and make a break with the past.

...a man came running up, greeted him with great reverence, and asked, "Good Teacher, what must I do to get eternal life?"

Jesus said, "Why are you calling me good? No one is good, only God. You know the commandments: Don't murder, don't commit adultery, don't steal, don't lie, don't cheat, honor your father and mother."

He said, "Teacher, I have—from my youth—kept them all!"

Jesus looked him hard in the eye—and loved him! He said, "There's one thing left: Go sell whatever you own and give it to the poor. All your wealth will then be heavenly wealth. And come follow me."

The man's face clouded over. This was the last thing he expected to hear, and he walked off with a heavy heart. He was holding on tight to a lot of things, and not about to let go.

Mark 10:17-22 (MSG)

You shut it down. You decide to kill it all off and start again.

It's not very popular these days, to talk about loss. Far better to talk about how Jesus can sprinkle the magic dust over the consequences of all the bad things I do, so that I can carry on smiling behind the mask, singing in church, as if nothing has really changed in my life. Use his forgiveness for when I mess up again and again in all the same ways with all the same people that I always have, because that's his job.

Amazing grace!

Everybody loves that.

But adding Jesus on to my life and then carrying on living the same way is not amazing grace. It's fake. It's what Dietrich Bonhoeffer, a German pastor who opposed Hitler, called 'cheap grace.'

> **CHEAP GRACE IS THE DEADLY ENEMY... GRACE WITHOUT PRICE; GRACE WITHOUT COST! THE ESSENCE OF GRACE, WE SUPPOSE, IS THAT THE ACCOUNT HAS BEEN PAID IN ADVANCE; EVERYTHING CAN BE HAD FOR NOTHING... THE WORLD FINDS A CHEAP COVERING FOR ITS SINS; NO CONTRITION IS REQUIRED, (OR) ANY REAL DESIRE TO BE DELIVERED FROM SIN.**
>
> **CHEAP GRACE IS GRACE WITHOUT DISCIPLESHIP, GRACE WITHOUT THE CROSS, GRACE WITHOUT JESUS CHRIST.**
>
> Dietrich Bonhoeffer, *The Cost of Discipleship*

You can't really add Jesus Christ and not **– SUBTRACT** all the bad habits, selfish acts, mean behaviour. You haven't got the real thing if you do that, just cheap grace. Jesus once asked,

> *"Why do you call me 'Lord, Lord' — and do not do what I say?"*
> Luke 6:46 (NIV)

He gave up his life for us. Our response is to give back our lives to him.

We have to let him **– SUBTRACT** the old life, so that we can have the new life.

It's wonderfully true that when you become a Christian — that is, a Jesus-follower — you become a new creation. You can live an extraordinary life! But let's not kid ourselves; if you do what you used to do, you'll have what you used to have. If you live the old life, you'll have the old life.

Too many people went to a church, liked the sound of all that love and acceptance, and later gave up on Christianity. If you ask them, it's because "It didn't work for me."

The real problem though was that it didn't work *in* them. It won't work for you if you won't let it work in you. What really counts is that you live it out every day — in all of your decisions. These people didn't work out their salvation. They wanted the additions, the bonuses, but no ➥ **SUBTRACTION**. It's a hard lesson, but what do you have to lose, to gain Jesus Christ?

Taking up the cross is not the easy life.

Still want to be a Christian?

Loser!

You might get snubbed at a party, laughed at on Facebook or called a 'Bible basher.' It hurts. But it's a small cross to bear. It hardly qualifies as persecution.

THEY LOVE ALL - AND ARE PERSECUTED BY ALL. THEY ARE UNKNOWN AND CONDEMNED; THEY ARE PUT TO DEATH AND RESTORED TO LIFE. THEY ARE POOR YET MAKE MANY RICH; THEY ARE IN LACK OF ALL THINGS AND YET ABOUND IN ALL; THEY ARE DISHONOURED AND YET IN THEIR VERY DISHONOUR ARE GLORIFIED. THEY ARE SPOKEN OF AS EVIL AND YET ARE JUSTIFIED; THEY ARE REVILED AND BLESS; THEY ARE INSULTED AND REPAY THE INSULT WITH HONOUR; THEY DO GOOD YET ARE PUNISHED AS EVILDOERS.

Description of Christians from *The Epistle of Mathetes to Diognetus* in the year 2 AD

Worldwide right now, Christians are statistically speaking by far the most persecuted religious body on the planet. According to the

International Society for Human Rights, 80 per cent of all acts of religious discrimination in the world today are directed at Christians.

A report published in *The Spectator* magazine shows that the world is witnessing the rise of an entire generation of Christian martyrs. Between 2006 and 2010 Christians faced discrimination in almost three-quarters of all the countries on Earth. An average of 100,000 Christians have been killed each year for the past decade and that figure is increasing exponentially in our day. That's 11 Christians losing their lives, somewhere in the world, every hour, seven days a week, 365 days a year, for reasons related to their faith.

Maybe you thought Jesus came to end all this conflict and strife, to make our lives happier, more safe and secure? Surely one of those names he was given in the Bible was Prince of Peace?

But Jesus didn't say that's how it would be. In **Matthew 10**, which I mentioned earlier, Jesus calls his disciples (which means those who learn) and tells them they are about to become apostles (which means those who are sent): off on a mission, for him. He tells them that God will provide everything they need and that they should expect miracles as they heal the sick, raise the dead and tell everyone there's a new King in town.

It's a scary task. He makes it even scarier in verse 16 when he says, **"you're going to be like sheep running through a wolf pack." (MSG)** That's not a comforting picture! Sheep are not known for their fighting skills. There are wolves! How does a sheep survive? Only by sticking very close to the shepherd....

Then he speaks beyond those disciples to all the rest of us, to anyone who will dare to become one of his sheep in a world full of wolves. He warns us to be ready for trials and tests, flogging and fleeing.

In verse 22 he tells them, *" You will be hated by everyone because of me!"* (NIV) Nobody's having that one put on a Christian bumper sticker, are they?

Jesus says this will happen to you. People are going to hate you.

Who? Who will hate me? He tells us in verse 21 that there will even be people in your own family.

Did you think you were signing up for that? Not just ➖ **SUBTRACTION** but division?

➗ DIVISION

What about all the love, joy and peace? Everyone happy together?

Then in verse 34, Jesus says this, **"Do not suppose that I have come to bring peace to the earth. I did not come to bring peace, but a sword."** (NIV) He describes brotherly betrayal, sisterly sellout and family fallout.

I HAVE COME TO BRING A SWORD

How does that mess up the popular picture of gentle Jesus, meek and mild? What does it mean that he's bringing a sword?

Well, when we hear sword we think 'violence.' Some of the Jews thought that they would be saved by a Messiah who would overthrow King Herod and rescue their nation from the hated Roman rulers. They would have known all about this from reading God's word since they were children, and dreaming of the warrior hero coming to make things right. They were looking for royalty, but Jesus told them time and again that yes, he was the king they were looking for, but no, that's not how he planned to rule.

What about peace? Jesus said he didn't come to bring it, yet he is described as the Prince of Peace. So what was he saying?

When we hear the word peace we have our own idea of what it means. A trouble-free life. Calm and quiet. No stress. Everyone getting on nicely. Apparently following Jesus won't lead to those outcomes.

The word for peace in Hebrew — and what all the people would have understood in those days — is *shalom*. Peace, *shalom*. It doesn't just mean no violence or an absence of noise. You could use it as a greeting: it's like saying "I hope you have the best possible life. Everything going well, fitting together nicely, with everyone happy and smiley." *Shalom* means 'complete.' Complete happiness here, having all you could want.

But Jesus said, "I've come to bring the opposite." What's the opposite of wholeness?

♣ DIVISION

Make no mistake. Following Jesus will bring ♣ **DIVISION**. The name of Jesus divides. Following Jesus divides. He's not about making everything respectable. He chucks a sword in.

Just try and say, "I'm not just trying to be a nice person: I know I do things wrong. The world needs a saviour, a rescuer. The only one qualified is Jesus, so I'm going to follow him no matter what. I'm going to take up my cross and live differently."

That will throw a sword in! It will get messy. ♣ **DIVIDE**, cut, sever in half.

You want a peaceful life? Tough. People won't like you following Jesus.

You don't want to stand out from the crowd? Jesus said that people-pleasing only leads you into trouble and compromise.

Did you hear the story of the Gordian Knot?

> "*There's trouble ahead when you live only for the approval of others, saying what flatters them, doing what indulges them. Popularity contests are not truth contests—look how many scoundrel preachers were approved by your ancestors! Your task is to be true, not popular.*"
>
> Luke 6:26 (MSG)

In Greek legend, a poor peasant called Gordias tied up his oxcart in the town square of Phrygia with a very complicated knot, with the ends tucked away on the inside.

Word was, that whoever released the knot would rule all of Asia. Many people who wanted to be king tried to undo the knot but with no success.

Over 100 years later, in 333 BC, at the tender age of 23, a guy called Alexander arrived at the town. He approached the cart as a crowd of curious townspeople gathered around. They watched him as he studied the knot for a little while. Then he stepped back and drew his sword, and in one stroke, he severed the knot. (This Alexander is known in history as Alexander the Great. So you can probably guess at whether he fulfilled those prophecies.)

He didn't mess about with it. He **÷ DIVIDED** it!

Now, sometimes life gets complicated. Relationships and decisions get complicated. We make our excuses and we want to be happy. We want to keep everyone happy. That makes it even more difficult, because we can't. Sometimes our choices end up tying us into things we never thought we'd be tied into. We can't seem to see or think of a way out.

Following Jesus could make it look even more complicated. He says uncomfortable things like he wants to be first. First before family, friends. First in everything.

For some people, following Jesus has meant **÷ DIVISION** before addition. Following Jesus has meant **— SUBTRACTION**. They had to lose some things. Some relationships, even. People who would hold them back from following. It's hard. It feels like taking up a cross. As that sword falls.

The amazing thing is, that **— SUBTRACTION AND ÷ DIVISION** are often God's path to addition. Because the cross changes everything. Jesus looked like the ultimate loser on the cross, but he beat it. The Bible says that he looked like a victim but he won the greatest victory.

There will come a time when everybody will recognise who Jesus is and what he has done. We don't know when but we do know that it's in God's plan. The cross has changed everything.

So yes, when you take up your cross, there's **— SUBTRACTION**.

When you take up your cross, there's ➗ *DIVISION*.

But you always get more than you thought you gave up. It's how God works.

Paul said, *"I've lost everything – to gain Christ."* Sometimes that's the way it has to be. You can't have both.

But when you lose, you can't lose.

Only you know how this could apply to you.

Your marriage, your morals, your money, your dating choices, your habits, how you raise your kids....

There could be ➖ *SUBTRACTION OR* ➗ *DIVISION* that needs to happen before God can bring the addition he wants to.

> *Think of yourselves the way Christ Jesus thought of himself. He had equal status with God but didn't think so much of himself that he had to cling to the advantages of that status no matter what. Not at all. When the time came, he set aside the privileges of deity and took on the status of a slave, became human! Having become human, he stayed human. It was an incredibly humbling process. He didn't claim special privileges. Instead, he lived a selfless, obedient life and then died a selfless, obedient death—and the worst kind of death at that—a crucifixion.*
>
> *Because of that obedience, God lifted him high and honoured him far beyond anyone or anything, ever, so that all created beings in heaven and on earth—even those long ago dead and buried—will bow in worship before this Jesus Christ, and call out in praise that he is the Master of all, to the glorious honour of God the Father.*
>
> *Philippians 2:5-11 (MSG)*

This is between you and God. He knows it all: it's ➖ *SUBTRACT* and ➗ *DIVIDE* time, because that has to happen before addition.

Nobody has ever regretted subtracting what Jesus called them to ➖ *SUBTRACT* . When you've given him that ➖ *SUBTRACTION*, willingly he will do the rest. Complete it. Turning your loss to gain, your letting go to living more than you could ever dream of. He wants to add so much more.

WORKOUT

I'm going to challenge you now: what do you need to **SUBTRACT?** Ask yourself honestly, is there someone or something that is holding you back, that you might need to separate your self from: **♣ DIVISION?** An influence that isn't helping you, a compromise?

That sword has to fall. On a habit, a pattern, a relationship that's got you tied up and tangled in its grip. Messy. You can't unravel it yourself. You can't untie it even if you tried. But you know exactly what it is.

My advice to you is: whatever you need to do, don't put it off. Before you turn the page — send the text, make the decision, draw the line.

CONNECT

Just listen to God's voice inside you, his Spirit speaking right now. Not shouting or bullying, but in a small voice, just saying, "Take up your cross. Lay down your life. Follow Jesus. Really. Deny yourself. Count it as loss. Die... to live. Stop playing games now."

Now tell him about your decision:

Thank you Jesus for taking up your cross and changing everything. I don't want anything to hold me back. Please help me to see what I need to let go, so that I can live in freedom.

✚ ADD

"Where your treasure is, your heart will be also."
Luke 12:34 (NIV)

You remember that story about Alexander the Great cutting through the Gordian knot in the city of Phrygia? Well another famous tale comes from that region, and it's one that we refer to now and then even today, to describe someone who seems to have amazing luck with money.

The time was the Eighth Century BC, and the setting a place which now forms part of Turkey. The ruler of the land was a man called King Midas, and he was incredibly wealthy. He had already amassed a great fortune, and loved nothing better than to count his gold.

The myth goes that King Midas was offered one wish. He didn't have to think twice. He asked for 'the golden touch.' The most ingenious way he could think of to ✚ *ADD* to his wealth even further was to have the power to turn everything he touched into pure gold.

He laid a trembling finger onto a bowl of fruit — immediately it was transformed and glittering. A gold chair, a gold wall!

"I'll have one of those!" he shouted as he pimped his chariot. "This one in gold!" as he bounded into the garden, touching a rose. "In fact, I'll add another, and another!"

What a gift!

And of course, that's the part of the story that we all remember: the Midas touch. How fantastic! Unlimited wealth — as much as you want! Happiness on tap.

But the story didn't end there. Because Midas began to realise the downside to having those magic fingers. Everything he touched included the food that he needed to eat. What do you do when your carrots turn into 24 carats?

Then, the worst part of all: excitedly he grasped his daughter's hand, saying, "Look what Daddy can do!" But she didn't follow. She had been turned into a perfect, life-size statue of a princess, cold and gold.

What had promised to be the key to happiness turned out to be the opposite. From elation to misery in a single touch.

The problem with getting what you think you want, is that you might not want what you get.

And of course, you can't keep it all anyway.

Fortunately for King Midas in this story, after he realised his mistake he got the chance to put it right. He was told to go to the River Pactolus, where he washed away his golden touch in the water, which supposedly now shimmers like gold....

You can't read any of the accounts of Jesus' life in the Bible without coming up against some really different attitudes to money and its place in our lives. Some of the challenges he put to people might make for uncomfortable reading for us today: about our values, our goals, our financial choices and our priorities. Most of the questions that Jesus was interested in boiled down to, "Who's the king? In your life, whose kingdom are you ✚ *ADDING* to?"

WHO'S THE KING OF THE CASTLE?

The stories that Jesus told about money showed God as the king, the 'owner' of the money. The word that Jesus used for us in our short time here on earth was 'steward' — someone who handles what belongs to another. Money belongs to the King of Heaven, and he owns it. We are accountable for what we do with it.

Today the world operates its economic system without acknowledging God. Everyone 'owns' their money. If I'm the owner of the money, then that makes me responsible for getting, protecting, worrying about and keeping what I own. It sounds very responsible, but actually, as we will see, it is faulty.

Most people's financial worldview can be described by the idea that there is a pie — a small pie — and there's only so much to go around. Who wins? He who has the most pie wins. At this period in history, a minority in a very few countries are eating all the pie. And suffering obesity problems. I live in the UK, which is one of the top ten of the world's richest countries, while the majority of the rest of the world find it hard to earn even a crust.

According to most people, the only way to help the poor is to encourage some people to create more wealth and hope they become more generous with that bit of extra pie. Maybe tax some pie off them, and encourage those who are hungry and without to be more inventive and hard-working so that they might be able to get a bit of pie themselves. At the end of it all, there's not enough for me and for you as well.

This view is called a scarcity mentality.

But the alternative the Bible would describe is that life is more like a river. God isn't running short on anything — it just keeps on coming. Remember that Jesus said he came so that we might have life, abundantly, more than enough to go around? There is plenty for everyone, if you're a river kind of person.

Here's another way of thinking about it. I visited the Dead Sea recently. A big stretch of water, 10 miles by 50 miles. You know why it's called the Dead Sea? There can be no life in it. It's the saltiest body of water on the planet, nine times saltier than the ocean.

And it's desolate. You'll never see a water skier on there. No holiday homes on the banks. The only people who like the Dead Sea are tourists, because it's impossible to sink in the water. So tour buses drive there, and you go bobbing in the water because the salt stops you sinking. It's fun to bob about (but man it burns in all your important little places...).

Why is it like that? There is fresh water flowing into the Dead Sea continuously, from the Jordan River and several other streams. But the Dead Sea has no outlet. And because it has no outlet, the fresh water comes in, and sits there, and the desert sun evaporates it all.

You know, it's possible to **✛ ADD**, **✛ ADD**, **✛ ADD** to me, me, me... and still be a dead person. In, in, in. To receive fresh resources, fresh blessings, fresh provisions from God on a regular basis. If there's no outlet, if you don't channel those resources out, out, out again: what's going to happen to you? No life!

Rivers have a source and they take the water from upstream and channel it downstream. You can do the same: take resources, money, that you have been given, and pass it all along. Be part of the flow, keeping it alive.

> **ARE YOU A RIVER PERSON OR A DEAD SEA PERSON?**

Now you might be thinking — all this talking about money is making me suspicious. I've heard the stories about those dodgy TV evangelists building up money for themselves. And you're right, because a gimme, gimme, gimme culture is the opposite of what I'm talking about right now.

I'm not talking about them and their big shiny cars, or even about me and my smaller, less shiny one. I'm talking about you. About your attitude to money. And the reason I'm doing it is not to try and trick you out of something, it's because Jesus did it. He talked about money a lot. Sometimes churches don't. They're so burnt by some of the huge greedy mistakes Christian people have made in the past that they just decide to ignore the issue. They limp along and can't do much for other people or change the world because, "We never talk about money." A badge of honour. "You won't hear about money here."

But Jesus talked about it all the time. Money is mentioned five times more than prayer in the Bible. Imagine a church saying, "We don't talk about prayer!"

The fact is, money is a big part of our lives, and it's not really possible to live on this earth without bumping into it at some point. Because of this, Jesus questioned people about their attitude to it, what they needed or wanted, how important they thought it was, how they were spending it. We're going to look at how he did that right now in *Luke 12:1-7*.

The scene begins with Jesus talking to his disciples — the friends who were following him around learning from him — although there was also a huge thousands-strong crowd of people swarming around, 'trampling on one another,' (verse 1) trying to catch his words. He was reminding them about the ➖ *SUBTRACTION* and ➗ *DIVISION* which was bound to come in their lives, but also encouraging them that all those things are nothing compared to the ✚ *ADDITION* of knowing him and staying on course with the life that he had planned for them. It must have been worrying to hear though, because he had to remind them of how God values them,

> *"Are not five sparrows sold for two pennies? Yet not one of them is forgotten by God. Indeed, the very hairs of your head are all numbered. Don't be afraid; you are worth more than many sparrows."*
>
> Luke 12: 6-7 (NIV)

See?! There he goes. Jesus talking about money... What are you worth? You are worth everything to God. You're unforgettable, always in his thoughts. You're priceless — he has a picture of you in his wallet!

Jesus might have talked about money, but that wasn't because he was worried about it. You're never going to read in the Bible, "And God said, 'No we can't afford that'," or "Jesus said, 'Listen friends, things are a bit tight right now'."

Jesus never had a scarcity mentality. He sent his disciples out to do the same works of miracles and healings as he was doing and told them, *"do not take a purse or bag" Luke 10:4 (NIV).* He wanted them to trust in God for the material things, so that they could focus on the ❯ *GREATER THAN*. And God did take care of them — they came back joyful! Everything Jesus did was in the confidence of knowing deep down that his Father God could be trusted to provide whatever was needed.

Now, Luke says that just as Jesus was teaching about why they shouldn't worry, someone from the crowd shouted out his worry: you can read it in *Luke 12:13-15 (NIV)*.

He wanted Jesus to step into his petty family argument about money and inheritance law, and of course to rule in his favour. "It's unfair! Awwww! Tell him to share!!"

> *Someone in the crowd said to him, "Teacher, tell my brother to divide the inheritance with me."*
>
> *Jesus replied, "Man, who appointed me a judge or an arbiter between you?" Then he said to them, "Watch out! Be on your guard*

against all kinds of greed; life does not consist in an abundance of possessions."

Luke 12:13-15 (NIV)

Jesus' response is, 'Don't even bother me with that.' Straight away he sees the real problem. The man is coming to Jesus with a money problem, and his definition of a money problem is that he doesn't have enough money, or he's not getting the money he thinks he deserves. But Jesus' point is, 'You do have a problem with money, but your problem is that money has too much of you.'

He warned everyone in the crowd about the dangers of greed, using the Greek word, *pleonexia*, a philosophical term about the insatiable feeling of wanting what others have and it never being enough.

GREED: IT EATS YOU UP.

Do you feel like you never have enough? That's a scarcity mentality.

Jesus told a story about where that feeling comes from, and where it ends up:

"The ground of a certain rich man yielded an abundant harvest. He thought to himself, 'What shall I do? I have no place to store my crops.'

"Then he said, 'This is what I'll do. I will tear down my barns and build bigger ones, and there I will store my surplus grain. And I'll say to myself, "You have plenty of grain laid up for many years. Take life easy; eat, drink and be merry".'

"But God said to him, 'You fool! This very night your life will be demanded from you. Then who will get what you have prepared for yourself?'

"This is how it will be with whoever stores up things for themselves but is not rich towards God."

Luke 12:16-21 (NIV)

In a lot of Bible translations, this particular story is headlined as The Parable [story] of the Rich Fool. But Jesus didn't give it that name, the Bible compilers did. I think Jesus would call it, The Story of Most

People. Or The Story of Anybody, Whoever. This could be your story. Or mine. If we're honest, we could all live like this.

Notice that it's not the story of how he became rich: he was rich at the start. He already had it all. He just didn't know when he had enough. Never thought he had enough. Not enough to be rich with. Then his land produced more. Abundantly. God gave him more than enough. But it didn't matter because he had a scarcity mentality.

How do I **PROTECT IT?** How do I **KEEP** it? How do I **HOARD** it and **STORE** it for tomorrow? How do I work, work, **WORK** for more, more, **MORE?** How can I enjoy myself with it? I'll be happy when I **✚ ADD** more. Maybe I'll be generous when I have more one day. One for me.... and another for me..... More for **ME**.

So he **✚ ADDED**. One barn, two barns, more barns... which equals... **ZERO**. Because he was dead.

The End.

Now most people who operate according to the scarcity worldview would call him a successful guy. That man collected all the pies. A financial genius. But he was only rich toward himself. He only laid up treasure for himself, where he could never keep it. So whatever the *Financial Times* obituary said about him, whatever they said at the funeral, God's verdict was that he was a fool.

They would say he was a go-getter. That's what he did. Go and get. Get, get, get. What did God say about him? A fool. You may get more money, but there's no way that you can extend your life one more minute, is there? When your time comes.

If we are only rich toward ourselves, we're financial fools.

But God's version of ✚ **ADDITION** isn't like that. He wants us to be wise men and women of great generosity. To be like Jesus, who said,

> *"It is more blessed to give than receive."*
> Acts 20:35 (NIV)

Do you think that Jesus believed that? Yes! Did he live like that verse was true? Yes! Do most people? No.

Jesus had a different mindset for many reasons, but one that strikes me is that he simply believed God is ❭ **GREATER THAN**. Remember that? Turning to his disciples as The Story of Most People sunk in, he told them again, "Don't worry!" And then he told them how to put money worries in their place.

You're not most people! God will take care of you. You are God's people so don't worry about what most people worry about. People who don't know him worry. You know him. **LIVE** like you do. **LOVE** like you do. **GIVE** like you do.

Did you know that above all else God is a giver? The most well-known verse in the Bible says, *"God so loved the world that he gave his only Son."* John 3:16 (NIV)

Aren't you glad God doesn't take his cues on giving from us? Wouldn't it be wonderful if we took our cues from him?

Earlier Luke records Jesus saying,

> *"Give, and it will be given to you. A good measure, pressed down,*

shaken together and running over, will be poured into your lap. For with the measure you use, it will be measured to you."

Luke 6:38 (NIV)

So, you give, and then you get back more.

If you give with a teaspoon, what are you getting back? If you give with a shovel, what are you getting back? You don't give to get back. You give because you're grateful and because it reflects the size of your heart for God — bigger than your heart for money.

When you give you never lose, and what you give you never lose. It's all you get to keep forever.

The way to not live like Most People is not to have more. It's to love more. Love God, and love people. He will make sure that there will always be enough for that. If you love what you have, you'll have what you love.

What I'm trying to do here is get you to relax, not be so preoccupied with getting so you can respond to God's giving. People who don't know God and the way he works fuss over these things, but you know both God and how he works. Steep yourself in God-reality, God-initiative, God-provisions. You'll find all your everyday human concerns will be met. Don't be afraid of missing out. You're my dearest friends! The Father wants to give you the very kingdom itself.

Be generous. Give to the poor. Get yourselves a bank that can't go bankrupt, a bank in heaven far from bank robbers, safe from embezzlers, a bank you can bank on. It's obvious, isn't it? The place where your treasure is, is the place you will most want to be, and end up being.

Luke 12:29-34 (MSG)

An ✚ *ADDITION* story...

I married my wonderful husband on a beautifully crisp December day, in a stunning designer wedding dress. I was the princess that I had always imagined I would look like on my wedding day and it felt incredible!

Not long after that I started working for a charity called The Message Trust. They held monthly prayer days, and it was at one of these that God spoke to me. I sat there, quite comfortably at first, listening to a couple of women share stories about some work they were doing in Uganda to support destitute women. They were setting up an enterprise business called Trade the Dress, which enabled the poorest of the poor to work by altering and selling donated wedding dresses. The income empowered them to feed and care for their families.

I tried not to cry as I realised God was asking me to donate my dress — only one year after I had walked down that aisle. I gave my dress that day to those women, not knowing who it would go to but trusting that God was going to use it to bless a wonderful bride who could never have afforded it, as well as create income for women who would otherwise be on the streets. It was not an easy thing to do, but I knew so clearly that I had to do it!

A year later, I sat with one of the leaders of the charity who explained how much the project had grown in Uganda, and we both realised that we'd love to see that happen where we live too. How amazing would it be to see disadvantaged couples and unemployed women here in the UK being blessed the way they were in Uganda through Trade the Dress?

We started meeting couples who were struggling financially, believing that they could never afford to get married at all, let alone foot the cost of an expensive dress. That's how The Wedding Angels began: now an organisation with a spectacular showroom, sewing apprentices, and incredible church partners.

Over the last two years we have supported twenty underprivileged couples, enabling them to stay out of debt at the start of their married life together by offering weddings at their budget. And guess what?... I now have over 100 stunning wedding dresses! On hearing our story, so many women have been inspired to do the same as I did by passing on their beloved dresses to a bride who thought she'd never be a princess. God has added more than we could ever have imagined, and matched my small gift a hundred times over.

Emma Jeffery, co-founder of *The Wedding Angels*

The answer to worry is not more money. It's more love, generosity, contentment and faith. God's river won't run dry. The sort of ✚ *ADDITION* that God works with is endless.

Jesus explained that living like this now in this life, God's river method of ✚ *ADDITION*, is the same as how it's done in heaven, in God's Kingdom. The ideal.

> *Seek first the kingdom of God... and all these things shall be added to you.*
>
> Matthew 6:33 (NIV)

✚ *ADDED*. To whom? To you. Do you want to add to you (scraped together for your own personal Dead Sea), or do you want God to add to you (with his unlimited river flow).

When you want what God wants, you can have what God has. And who has more to give? You, or God? This is the opposite of the scarcity mentality. This is the **ABUNDANCE** mentality: there is always going to be more than enough, so what can we do to share it?

Paul wrote a letter to encourage people in Corinth to live great big, cheerfully generous lives. He explained,

> *"God can pour on the blessings in astonishing ways so that you're ready for anything and everything, more than just ready to do what needs to be done."*
>
> 2 Corinthians 9:8 (MSG)

Generosity starts and scarcity stops when we fix our eyes on the ❭ *GREATER THAN* God. A God who can.

Do you believe that is true? Enough to live like it? Prove it today!

If we prove what we believe by how we behave, who knows what might happen? Imagine if we actually behaved like we believed this? How would we live? More than ready for astonishing things?

We'd live like Jesus. Jesus' life was all about setting people free. Peter summed it up as:

> *'He went about doing good and, in particular, curing all who were harassed and oppressed by the power of the devil, for God was with Him.'*

Acts 10:38 (AMP)

He did that because God was his dad, and the source of everything he needed. He knew there was plenty more where that came from. Always enough!

Enough bread to feed an enormous crowd, enough power to heal, enough fish to break all the nets, and sometimes just exactly the right amount of money to pay the tax bill, found in the most unusual place. Really. You can find all those events in the gospels written by Jesus' friends, and many more besides. He knew what people needed and he was able to provide.

Are you a getter, a hoarder, a taker? Or are you a giver?

> *The world of the generous gets larger and larger, the world of the stingy person gets smaller and smaller.*
>
> King Solomon (one of the richest men in history) in Proverbs 11:24 (MSG)

There is so much more life in the river than in the Dead Sea.

However good they are at maths and economics, people with a scarcity mentality will always be afraid of giving because they see it as ▬ **SUBTRACTION**, not investment: ✚ **ADDITION**. They think they will lose when they give, but the truth is that what you give becomes the thing that you can never lose.

Which world do you live in? Are you empire building for you, or kingdom building for God?

Are you grimly ✚ **ADDING** to your own personal Dead Sea, barnfuls and armfuls of stuff that you can't take with you? Watching it all stagnate while you wait?

Or are you ready to plunge into the river and start being generous? Because you know that God will always give you what you need, and you can have the confidence to start sharing it all around. Poured out and running over....

WORKOUT

Being generous can start right away. It's about the attitude. Start small but aim big!

Do you have some clothes that you don't wear that much? How about donating them to your local charity shop? Do it now — open your cupboard and see if you can find a few items (you probably won't even miss them).

Make a cake for your neighbours.

Sponsor a child who lives in poverty: you can donate a small amount each month and they will be able to eat and go to school. Check out how it works at Compassion **compassionuk.org**

Donate food to your local Foodbank. You can find out more here **trusselltrust.org/get-involved**

Look out for ways to be generous, each day. The opportunities are endless. Take them, and start seeing what God will do.

CONNECT

Father God, thank you that I can trust you with the small things like money, so that I can get on with the big things, doing the stuff that Jesus did while he was here on earth.

I don't want to get distracted by greed. Help me to have a giving attitude, and show me where you want me to be generous in my life. Help me to have a bigger heart for you.

∞ INFINITY

"*I give them* **ETERNAL** *life, and they shall never perish; no one will snatch them out of my hand.*"

John 10:28 (NIV)

There's a story which an author called Somerset Maugham once told, about a rich businessman living in Baghdad.

He sent his servant to do some shopping in the market, but a little while later the servant came back, white and trembling. "Master!" he said, "Just now when I was in the marketplace I was jostled by someone in the crowd — and when I turned I saw it was Death. She looked at me and made a threatening gesture. Lend me your horse, and I will ride away from this city to avoid my fate. I will go to Samarra. Death will never find me there."

So his master lent him the horse, and the servant dug his spurs in its flanks and raced away as fast as the horse could gallop. Then the businessman went down to the marketplace, and sure enough, he saw Death standing in the crowd. He went up to Death, and demanded, "Why did you make a threatening gesture to my servant when you saw him this morning?"

"That was not a threatening gesture," said Death, "It was a start of surprise. I was astonished to see him here in Baghdad, because I have an appointment with him tonight in Samarra."

> ## DEATH IS THE DEBT WE MUST ALL PAY
>
> **Euripides**

We all have an appointment in Samarra! Our time is always getting shorter. Someday, our meeting with Death will come. Death is the one thing that we all share in common.

I got on a plane last week, and from the moment he sat down, I could see that the guy next to me, a great big lad, was scared to death. He'd obviously had to medicate before he'd got on the plane. With beer. He wanted more all the way from Southampton to Manchester. He was really shaking.

I asked him, "Why are you so scared?"

He said, "Well, what if we're all going to die?"

I said, "We are. We are all going to die. But probably not now."

I thought that was quite a good joke, but looking back, I can see why it didn't help calm him down. So I decided to be a bit more sensitive (I am a pastor after all), so I got talking to him to take his mind off it.

I said, "Don't worry, you're in the second safest seat on the plane."

He brightened up: "What — statistically speaking?"

"No, biblically speaking. I work for God, and I believe he still has lots of things for me to do in Manchester. He's going to get me there safe. I'm in this seat. This seat is going to Manchester. You're in the seat next to me."

It became a great opportunity to share what I believe about God with him because he was 100% focused (well, maybe 70% because of the beer) and because I wasn't scared.

I don't mean not scared of flying. I mean I'm not scared of dying. I'm not saying I particularly want to do so today necessarily, but for me, as a Jesus follower, it's not the worst that can happen. The worst thing that can happen is never coming alive.

It's funny really how, if you're honest, you don't allow yourself to think about dying until you get on a plane. You don't think that when you get on a bus, do you? When you look at some of the buses and how they get driven, maybe you should!

Are you scared to death of death? There's a word for that: *thanataphobia.*

Years ago there was a documentary on TV about Michael Jackson. It was a big thing because he actually allowed the interviewer, Martin Bashir, into his home. Remember where he lived? Neverland. The cameras followed him as they toured the rooms, zooming in on all the amazing features. Around the house there were lots of statues of Peter Pan.

Bashir asked Jackson, "Why are you so interested in Peter Pan?"

Jackson answered, "I am Peter Pan. I never want to grow up."

Even so he seemed obsessed about aging and death. Bashir pointed to a display of coffins in a mall and asked, "Do you want to be buried or cremated?" Jackson replied, "I don't want to die. I want to live forever."

When Richard Branson was once asked how he wanted to be remembered, he said, "I don't want to be remembered. I want to be here!"

But all the money and power and influence can't make that happen. We might be used to being in control, and here in the West we've been able to control so much. Astonishing progress in technology, medicine and communication has been made in the past few decades. But we still can't control death.

Death is the last taboo subject. It's something you really shouldn't discuss in polite company. We say, "She's passed away," because 'dead' sounds too brutal and final.

The two main jobs I've worked have made me familiar with death. I saw my first dead body when I was sixteen. In the police, I saw murder victims, car crash deaths, even the Manchester Airport disaster.

But it's not just the shocking deaths is it? As a minister I've held hands with countless grieving family members who have lost their child, mum, dad, husband or wife. That look on their faces: "The world just changed totally. We don't know what to do. How can we go on now?"

Some people don't go on. They stop — 'stop all the clocks,' like the poem says — make a shrine perhaps, freeze the moment. Some people shake a fist toward heaven, others open up their hands for help. How do you deal with death?

To be honest, I don't know how anyone not closely connected to God, with a different, eternal perspective, copes at times like this. If death really is the end of the world.

What do you think happens next? Do you have a view of life that can

> ## HERE LIES AN ATHEIST. ALL DRESSED UP AND NO PLACE TO GO
>
> *Found on a headstone in a cemetery in Thurmont, Maryland*

cope with the inevitability of ∞ *INFINITY?*

Do you have a view of time big enough to cover eternity? Bible believers see Time as we know it — the short passage from life and death — as just a dot on eternity. They see this life as just a test, a trial, a trust. The warm up, practice lap, for the forever that God has prepared for us.

Not everyone believes that of course. Maybe you don't. But we're all going to die. So — what do we do?

IGNORE DEATH?

Mary Baker Eddy, the founder of a cult called Christian Science, once wrote, "There is no sin, sickness, nor death." Then she died. Bummer.

One of the most common poems read at funerals these days is called *Death is Nothing At All*. Have you heard it?

> ### DEATH IS NOTHING AT ALL. I HAVE ONLY SLIPPED AWAY TO THE NEXT ROOM.
>
> Excerpt from *Death Is Nothing At All* by Henry Scott Holland

It makes me want to get up and shout, "NO!" Death is something! We are not the same. That's why these people are grieving. We'd love to just walk next door and talk again with the person, but we can't, and that's why it hurts! Ignoring the reality doesn't make it any easier.

Jesus didn't ignore death. He was never afraid to talk about it. Not even his own death. It seems he spent much of his life knowing when and how he would die — which was in his early thirties. He wasn't morbid at all, yet he predicted it in detail. He never ignored it or denied it. He tried to prepare his friends for it. On one occasion he brought up the subject as they were on a journey.

> Jesus and his disciples headed out for the villages around Caesarea Philippi. As they walked, he asked, "Who do the people say I am?"
>
> "Some say 'John the Baptizer,'" they said. "Others say 'Elijah.' Still others say 'one of the prophets.'"

He then asked, "And you—what are you saying about me? Who am I?"

Peter gave the answer: "You are the Christ, the Messiah."

Jesus warned them to keep it quiet, not to breathe a word of it to anyone.

Mark 8: 27-30 (MSG)

Peter had a revelation — he recognised who Jesus actually is. All the disciples would have known that the Christ, the Messiah, was the promised one who was going to rescue them, and that he would come to change life forever. When Peter said that, he was saying that he knew that Jesus was the Son of God. He suddenly recognised him for who he was.

And Jesus didn't say to him, "Oh no Peter, calm down, I'm just a teacher, just a man trying to be good, just an example." He said, "Keep what you know about me to yourself for now; and I'll tell you what's going to happen next..."

He then began explaining things to them:

"It is necessary that the Son of Man proceed to an ordeal of suffering, be tried and found guilty by the elders, high priests, and religion scholars, be killed, and after three days rise up alive." He said this simply and clearly so they couldn't miss it.

Mark 8:31-32 (MSG)

The Greek word used for 'simply and clearly' is *parresia* which means 'exactly, explicitly.' It wasn't a figure of speech, a picture or a metaphor.

Jesus didn't ignore death. We can't afford to either.

Another way we might handle death is to **GET MYSTICAL**.

Tell a few stories out of your imagination to make it all seem a bit more rosy. We put flowers around the grave to disguise the reality. Maybe we're all part of *The Circle of Life*, like the Lion King. When you die, you feed the worms: but wouldn't it be nicer if you come back as a worm, or a bird that eats worms, or even better, a cat?

How about being a ghost? A butterfly? A star to watch over your loved ones?

But that's not how Jesus presented it. Peter was indignant when Jesus predicted his own death. He didn't want to hear it. It wasn't a nice parable (a story that Jesus often told to explain things to people) or a helpful illustration. It was too much information!

So when Jesus said,

"I'm really going to die, and then physically rise again. It's God's way." Peter only hears the bit about dying, and reacts.

> But Peter grabbed him in protest. Turning and seeing his disciples wavering, wondering what to believe, Jesus confronted Peter. "Peter, get out of my way! Satan, get lost! You have no idea how God works."

> Mark 8:32-33 (MSG)

Peter responds with, "No way! No way are you going to die!" His focus, all he could see, was, "How is this going to affect me, now?" He couldn't see beyond that grief. His loss, his fear, his pain.

He couldn't see the bigger picture. Focused on the here and now, close up. Conversely, Jesus had the wide angle lens and saw the there and then of eternity.

Peter had realised that Jesus was the Messiah, and he had been taught at school that this Messiah was going to be part of an amazing rescue. Rescue for all the Jewish people trapped by Roman rulers. Rescue for their nation to be free again! Holy people had been predicting it for generations: you can actually see hundreds of such predictions earlier in the Old Testament, which was their Bible. It's just that they'd got the wrong idea about rescue. They thought it was for their nation, for their people, at a specific time in history.

They didn't realise that it was a far bigger battle that Jesus was fighting. They didn't realise that he had come to rescue everyone, and everything, everywhere!

In the strongest terms that you can imagine, Jesus said, "Yes I do have to die! And it's you who is completely wrong. I'm not letting Satan get in the way. Stop trying to deflect me from my mission." Jesus saw his death from God's perspective. Peter saw it from a human perspective. Peter didn't know what Jesus was doing. Jesus knew exactly what he was doing.

Jesus' mission is summed up brilliantly in Hebrews:

> *"Since the children are made of flesh and blood, it's logical that the Saviour took on flesh and blood in order to rescue them by his death. By embracing death, taking it into himself, he destroyed the Devil's hold on death and freed all who cower through life, scared to death of death."*

Hebrews 2: 14-15 (MSG)

The mission that Jesus took on? Meet death; defeat death.

It's interesting: we run to things in life that seem to offer a bit more life, but many of them lead to death. And we run away from death because it scares us. What if it kills us?!?

Jesus embraced death. Why? Because he was going to kill it.

As the Son of God, Jesus was able to absorb death into himself in one eternal moment. Soaked it up inside him like a sponge. There on the cross, with all the things we ever did wrong, all our shame, all our sickness, all our shortcomings.

A couple of months after this, after everything he predicted had happened exactly as he'd said, and those prophecies from earlier in the Bible had all come true, right to the letter... there was a change amongst that scared little band of followers.

> *"It is finished."*
> *Jesus' words as he died on the cross, John 19:30 (NIV)*

Seeing Jesus arrested, rejected, killed, but beating death; seeing him come alive again and go back to heaven to be with his Father God stirred something — an understanding of God's ∞ **INFINITY** in their hearts : hope rose with him.

Then, once Jesus had left the earth, God sent his own Spirit, full of power, to all his followers. They became strong and brave because they were starting to see things like God did. From the perspective of ∞ **INFINITY**.

The lambs became lions. Including Peter. The same Peter who tried to divert Jesus from that scary path to death, who couldn't own up to even knowing Jesus once he'd been arrested, who just hadn't got the ∞ **INFINITY** view, was suddenly transformed.

Straight after he got that powerful gift of God's Spirit, Peter stood to address a massive crowd. He looked around, eyeballed some there who were involved in crucifying his master, and told everyone what had happened. "You killed him, God raised him, we saw him!" Not some nice stories or ideas. The fact that Jesus died to beat death for us, and rose again so that we don't need to be scared any more.

> *"...listen to this: Jesus of Nazareth was a man accredited by God to you by miracles, wonders and signs, which God did among you through him, as you yourselves know. This man was handed over to you by God's deliberate plan and foreknowledge; and you, with the help of wicked men, put him to death by nailing him to the cross. But God raised him from the dead, freeing him from the agony of death, because it was impossible for death to keep its hold on him."*

Acts 2:22-24 (NIV)

You think that life after death is impossible? No! I'll tell you what was impossible — it was impossible for death to beat Jesus! Death couldn't hold him. So death is defeated.

Death, once so dreadful and all-encompassing, the decay that creeps up little by little and grips us. Death, boasting because it never lost — Satan's master plan to destroy God's Son forever. Death was going down.

That day when Peter was arguing with Jesus, he was firmly planted on this earth, thinking like a human. Once he saw and understood what Jesus was talking about, death lost its sting, and ∞ **INFINITY** beckoned. God's eternity view showed death for what it was.

When Jesus first started out on his ministry — touring around and telling people all the news he had to tell them about God's plan — he went into the desert to pray and talk to God alone. You can read it in **Matthew 4:1-11**. While he was there, Satan came along to try and derail it all. He tried to tempt Jesus by offering him all the kingdoms of the earth, if he'd just bow down and worship him. No need for a cross. A pain-free, problem-free life.

"Not good enough!" Jesus said. "I made all that anyway, and I don't need to believe your lies or fall in with your ways to get it all back." He had something far better in mind than his own, earthly life. He was thinking of where he had come from and where he was going. He was thinking of **∞ INFINITY**.

I saw a sympathy card the other day that read, 'We all started out the same way and we'll all end up the same way.' Nice idea. It's another way people try to handle death. In theological terms it's called **UNIVERSALISM**. It's a really tolerant view, because it says that if you're sincere, no matter what you believe, or refuse to believe, no matter what you do or don't do; even if you've lived life as if you blatantly don't want to go there, you too will end up in heaven.

Oh, unless of course you're 'a really bad person.'

But who draws that line? If it's down to who's bad and who's good? What if you're nearly bad, but not quite? What if you're nearly good, but not quite? What if we're drawing the line wrong anyway, and it's not a vertical one between good and bad people, but a horizontal one between everyone and God?

People won't like it if you question this one, because it seems so fair. But is it really?

Jean-Paul Sartre, the philosopher, once said that death is only threatening if you think of it as personal: your death. If you think of it as a concept, a thing not related to you, then it's fine.

But should you keep death at a distance? If you know that one day you are going to face it — and you are! — wouldn't it be better to think about this ahead of time?

So, if I'm doing my job properly I need to do this, even if it makes us both uncomfortable, I'm going to ask you: what about you?

What belief system do you have about life and death — and where is it taking you? Make no mistake, you have a belief system, and it's taking you somewhere. The test of a belief system about death is not simply in how you live it out, but in whether it outlives you.

What the disciples heard — and eventually found the courage to live out — was that what you believe really is a matter of life and death.

At the end of that revelation conversation we were looking at earlier, Jesus put it all in context.

> *"If any of you wants to be my follower, you must turn from your selfish ways, take up your cross, and follow me. If you try to hang on to your life, you will lose it. But if you give up your life for my sake and for the sake of the Good News, you will save it. And what do you benefit if you gain the whole world but lose your own soul? Is anything worth more than your soul?"*

Mark 8:34-37 (NLT)

Read that again as if your life depends upon it — because it does! It's decision time. Do you see that sentence, from when we were working on **SUBTRACT AND ÷ DIVIDE?** 'Take up your cross and follow me.' For a lot of the early Christians it turned out to be literal, they really did end up dying. But the fact was, they didn't see death as the most frightening thing anymore, because they were looking at it from an **∞ INFINITY** point of view.

WHAT WE DO NOW ECHOES IN ETERNITY.

From The Meditations of Marcus Aurelius

I remember sitting in the car with a friend who had never quite seemed ready to commit his life to Jesus... 'just yet.' Like he'd be too ashamed to say to the lads he played football with that he belonged to Jesus. He asked me, "Do Christians face death better?" I thought a while before answering.

"The people I've known who knew Jesus best had the most security about death and were free to live life to the full, even when they knew they were going to die."

There are many philosophies or systems people come up with to deal with death. But whether they deny it, worship it, or come up with a plan to delay it, at the end it comes down to two options. Only two.

And there's a historical event which sums them up perfectly.

The sinking of The Titanic. Did you see the film? One of the big themes is the difference between rich and poor. Kate Winslet's rich girl meets Leonardo DiCaprio's poor cheeky chappie, Jack. There were dances and spectacular luxury for the first class passengers, while down below on their way to the deepest decks, people were being checked for fleas before being allowed on. As well as the 'haves' and the 'have-nots', there were also famous celebrities and people who were unknown; young people and old people. So many differences!

I went to a museum exhibition about the sinking of The Titanic. We went as a family. As we walked in, we were all given a ticket with a name on it. They were the names of the people who had been on the ship on that journey. We looked around the different cabins, saw some actual artefacts from the wreck, and then, as we left, you got to check your name on a list to see whether your passenger had made it. I was the only one who had drowned, apparently. Typical.

Now, when The Titanic sank, newspapers worldwide printed two columns side by side. Ultimately, it came down to these two columns. One list was titled 'Saved' and the other, 'Lost.'

Two eternal categories. You can get distracted by all the other things that seem important, like being rich, famous, young, attractive. But this ship is going down, and when it does, you'll either be saved or lost.

> # THE TITANIC IS A METAPHOR OF THE INEVITABILITY OF DEATH. WE'RE ALL ON THE TITANIC.
>
> James Cameron, movie director of The Titanic

Two options. Saved and lost. It's the church's job to tell people that they have a choice.

> "I am the Living One; I was dead, and now look, I am alive forever and ever! And I hold the keys of death and Hades."
>
> Revelation 1:18 (NIV)

The greatest tragedy about death is not dying. It's that so many people don't know the one who chose death, so that we can choose life! Jesus died for us, blotting out everything we've done wrong, and rose again as our Saviour. The one who saves us. Without him, I have no hope.

There was a great preacher in the late 1800s called Charles Spurgeon. In one of his talks — they were packed, thousands of people went — he challenged everyone to go home from the meeting and write down on a piece of paper which of the two categories they put themselves into. "Just write one word, 'saved' or 'lost'."

One man was angry at the idea that not everyone would go to heaven, and he decided to go home and write the word 'lost' on his paper, to spite the preacher and make a point to this unfair God. At home, raging at his desk, he pulled out his pen to write. His young daughter saw that he had already formed the letter 'L.'

> A bystander said, "Master, will only a few be saved?" He said, "Whether few or many is none of your business. Put your mind on your life with God. The way to life—to God!—is vigorous and requires your total attention."
>
> Luke 13:23-24 (MSG)

She begged him, "No, Daddy, don't write that! Just ask God to save you. Ask Jesus to save you!" The man wrestled with himself, before seeing the love of God reflected in his little girl's eyes. He broke down and asked God to forgive, save and lead him, from that day on and for eternity. And he was saved.

I don't know how many people will be saved by Jesus. I think it will be more than people try and calculate. But this choice is not about other people. You can't work out someone else's salvation.

Outside of a relationship with Jesus Christ, there's no hope of a cure for this terminal disease, the one we'll all suffer from eventually: death. If God points that out, it's not because he doesn't love you. A doctor has to tell you the diagnosis before you'll accept the treatment. Then you'll do what he says. He'd do you no favours by not hurting your feelings and letting you die.

Remember Jesus' conversation with his disciples, where Peter is only seeing the short term pain? One of Jesus' points was, "Don't gain the world and lose your soul." Bad swap! Your decision makes all the difference, and there are only two categories. Are you still lost in the here and now? Or are you safe in the promise of God's ∞ **INFINITY?**

Choose! Choose now! When this life ends, you don't just get back on the merry-go-round: *'people are destined to die once, and after that to face judgment...'* Hebrews 9:27 (NIV)

You too have an appointment in Samarra. Only a fool would go all through life unprepared for something he or she knows is inevitably going to happen. One day you're going to stand before God. Your life, too, is going to end.

And the question is not, "Will I live forever?" Everyone is going to live forever, after they have died on this Earth. The question is "Where? Where will you live forever?"

Where will you spend eternity? It all rises and falls on that one decision: to be saved or lost.

The only categories that count are 'Saved with Christ' or 'Lost without him.'

> ## WE'RE ALL GOING TO DIE!!!!
> *Screamed in any disaster movie, ever*

No second chances when you get to that day. But now you do have a chance. Why not ask him today?

 **WORK OUT**

Which category do you fall into? Lost or saved. Make your decision today.

Write it here:

_____

Your life depends upon this! It's the most important thing you will ever do.

 **CONNECT**

Jesus, thank you that you stared death down and then broke its power on the cross. You came to save me from the fear of death. I want to get to know you. I want to put my faith in you. I want to lead others to you, so that they can get to know you too. I'm not ashamed to say it, I'm excited about what this means for my life. I'm in this now for **∞ INFINITY**.

Forever Yours

_____

[Signed]

X MULTIPLY

"...go and make disciples of all nations...."
Matthew 28:19 (NIV)

When Jesus was first setting out on his earth mission, aged about 30, he looked about for some people to work with him. It wasn't a long and complicated interview process, just a simple request. No song and dance. One invitation... to change a life. Here's how he did it:

> As Jesus was walking beside the Sea of Galilee, he saw two brothers, Simon called Peter and his brother Andrew. They were casting a net into the lake, for they were fishermen. 'Come, follow me,' Jesus said, 'and I will send you out to fish for people.' At once they left their nets and followed him.
>
> Going on from there, he saw two other brothers, James son of Zebedee and his brother John. They were in a boat with their father Zebedee, preparing their nets. Jesus called them, and immediately they left the boat and their father and followed him.
>
> Matthew 4:18-22 (NIV)

He was saying, "Follow me." But also, "I will make you into something that you're not, yet."

Now there are many things I might wish or hope following Jesus would make me.

I wish he'd said, "Come and follow me and I will make you a great cook." I wish he'd said, "Come and follow me and I will make you cleverer." "Come and follow me, and I will make you rich... or good at football... or great at singing."

If I was writing the list of things that I'm not, those things would be up there. And there's a long list of things that I'm not.

But Jesus didn't promise that if I follow him I will become good at diving, DIY or disco dancing.

He said, "Follow me and I will make you — something that naturally you are not. I will make you — fishers of people."

Jesus puts this top of the list of things we need to be. Something that isn't stuck in the here and now, but will make a difference for ever: the **∞ INFINITY** perspective. Helping people find their way back to God. That's the job description. Go out fishing in the world. You're not trawling for tiddlers, but aiming to pull in some six-footers.

You will **✗ MULTIPLY** what God has done in your life, by giving that invitation to others. "Follow him!"

It's not just about making yourself a better person — although you will see some side effects there too — this is about a far bigger goal. Changing people's identity from Lost to Saved. From Perishing to Purposeful.

Look at this story that Jesus told about **✗ MULTIPLICATION**:

> Then he told them many things in parables, saying: "A farmer went out to sow his seed. As he was scattering the seed, some fell along the path, and the birds came and ate it up. Some fell on rocky places, where it did not have much soil. It sprang up quickly, because the soil was shallow. But when the sun came up, the plants were scorched, and they withered because they had no root. Other seed fell among thorns, which grew up and choked the plants. Still other seed fell on good soil, where it produced a crop – a hundred, sixty or thirty times what was sown. Whoever has ears, let them hear."
>
> *Matthew 13:3–9 (NIV)*

His disciples were getting a little confused with all the parables, and asked Jesus for a straight explanation, and so he gave it:

> "Listen then to what the parable of the sower means: when anyone hears the message about the kingdom and does not understand it, the evil one comes and snatches away what was sown in their heart. This is the seed sown along the path. The seed falling on rocky ground refers to someone who hears the word and at once receives it with joy. But since they have no root, they last only a short time. When trouble or persecution comes because of the word, they quickly fall away. The seed falling among the thorns refers to someone who hears the word, but the worries of this life and the deceitfulness of wealth choke the word, making it unfruitful. But the seed falling on good soil refers to someone who hears the word

and understands it. This is the one who produces a crop, yielding a hundred, sixty or thirty times what was sown."

Matthew 13:18-23 (NIV)

Jesus wants you to be the 'good soil,' and the litmus test is that it produces many times what was sown. Not just one seed, choking amongst the worries and ambitions of this world, but a crop: ✘ *MULTIPLIED*.

How does that work? How do we ✘ *MULTIPLY?* And notice how high Jesus' expectation is: as much as a hundred times!

Personally, I'd pretty much do anything to tell people about Jesus. I have done all kinds of things since I became a Christian.

When I was in the police, my first foray into trying to 'fish for people' was to wear a fish badge.

You may not have seen one of these (there was a definite trend for them at one point a few years ago among Christians). The fish symbol began as a sort of code for the early Christians back in Roman times, when life as a believer was highly dangerous. The letters for 'fish' in the version of the Greek language that they spoke at that time: ICHTHYS, spelt out the first letters of the phrase 'Jesus Christ, God's Son, Saviour.' Nearly 2000 years later, I wanted to get in on this. So I wore a fish badge on the tie of my uniform. Because I'd just become a Christian.

I played out scenes in my head where, one night in a Panda car, some spiritually troubled fellow officer would ask me in a quiet way, "Hey, I've always wondered what those fish badges meant — can you explain it, so behold I too can repent and be saved, or something?" I had my reply all ready for this situation and rehearsed it to myself.

Funnily enough, it didn't happen.

Nobody noticed. Nobody asked. For months, until one day, I walked into a room full of about one hundred hairy police officers. Everyone was facing the Inspector at the front, who suddenly lifted his hand and pointed, straight at me and my fish badge. Every eye in the place swivelled to look at me.

"Delaney! That fish..."

Oh no. The little Christian fish! I'd completely forgotten about it! Suddenly it seemed to be about ten feet long and flapping on my tie.

This was it. The moment of my death. I had been chosen as a martyr for the faith. Forced to declare my new-found allegiance to Christ. I could feel the flames already. If they didn't throw me out the window, at the very least these guys would be taking the mickey until next year. What could I say? After an eternal pause, the Inspector spoke again.

"I didn't know you were into angling! I run the angling section, come and see me later and I'll get you signed up."

I breathed again.

But that was when I decided that a car sticker was a far better option.

I had seen all sorts of Christian car stickers. So I got one: a fish. But nobody noticed or asked about it, either. So I got a rainbow fish and put that next to it. Then I got one that said, "Don't follow me, follow Jesus!" I pretty much went Christian car sticker crazy.

One day I saw the guy in front of me had nearly as many Christian car stickers as I had. Yes! Finally someone who wasn't scared to show it! But the problem was, he didn't realise about my sticker collection, because I was behind him. I had to let him know.

Looking back, the blind bend ahead and aggressive overtaking move probably weren't the best way to share my zeal for the faith. It took all my police driver's course training, a foot flat to the floor and the fact that one of my car stickers said, "Angels on board" not to cause an accident. (I realise now that the "Jesus is my co-pilot" sticker would not have helped me in court: yes, he took the penalty, but the points would have gone on *my* licence.)

Straightening up on the road in front of my new fellow Christian brother I took a glance in the rear view mirror to see if he'd clocked our shared interests. Strangely, though, the only communication from him seemed to involve two fingers, and other gestures I hadn't ever associated with prayers of blessing.

That was when Zoe decided that we didn't need Christian car stickers in the car any more. Apparently I drove more like a gladiator than a Christian.

A few years later, I got involved with some work in local high schools to help young people find their way back to God. We decided that a few magic tricks would liven up my talks, then I thought that some juggling exploits might catch people's attention, so I taught myself that as well. I figured, I'll do anything if it means that someone might listen and change their mind about God.

I even learnt fire eating. Until one day, on the back of a float on a parade in Nottingham, the wind blew the flames the wrong way, and I then had to do a talk to a bunch of mocking teenagers with my eyelashes stuck together and my fringe and eyebrows burnt off. Another time I nearly died.

That was when Zoe decided that the fire-eating had to stop. Overall probably a good plan, as you can't help people to find their way back to God when you're dead.

I've preached out in the street lots of times, all over the world.

I used to wear those ridiculous vicar dresses, and cheesy Christian t-shirts with messages on.

The reason I do it is because I have come to know the love of God, how amazing he is, his power, love, grace, guidance and generosity so freely, I want to do what Jesus said, and **✗ MULTIPLY** with my influence wherever I can.

I will do pretty much anything to tell people about him. To fish for people. But the population of the world is exploding, and we simply can't print enough t-shirts or leave it to the men in frocks to get this message out. Honestly, that's a very slow way to **✚ ADD**, never mind **✗ MULTIPLY** . So, what's the best way to help all those lost people find their way back to God?

Recently I spoke at a conference, and before my session, they interviewed a pastor from South East Asia. His name is Ying Kai, and he was born in Taiwan. His dad was a pastor too, and so from an early age, everyone assumed he was a Christian. If they asked him, he would reply, "I am a pastor's son." and that seemed to convince them.

One day though, a missionary saw through this backseat faith, and challenged him: "God doesn't have grandchildren. You might be a pastor's son, but are you a follower of Jesus Christ?" Kai realised he needed to make a decision for himself, so that night, at the age of 12, he knelt down, and in a moment he described as total surrender, he said, "Jesus, come into my heart. You can have my life, I will serve you wherever you want me to."

Since then, he has started 140,000 church communities, mostly in China. The movement he leads has baptised over 1.7 million new believers, all across China, India, and in various other nations around the world. This isn't just ✗ **MULTIPLICATION**, it's **EXPONENTIAL**[x] growth!

So they asked him, "How do you do it? How do you make such an impact? Especially in places where it's so hard and Christians can be persecuted? What's your system?"

I had my pen poised, because after all my attempts over the years, I was impatient for what Ying Kai was going to say. The answer to how you reach so many people.

He said that the strategy is simple. In fact, it turns out I knew it already, because it's found in what Jesus said just before he headed back to heaven and left this ✗ **MULTIPLYING** business in our hands:

> *Then Jesus came to them and said, "All authority in heaven and on earth has been given to me. Therefore go and make disciples of all nations, baptising them in the name of the Father and of the Son and of the Holy Spirit, and teaching them to obey everything I have commanded you. And surely I am with you always, to the very end of the age."*

Matthew 28:18-20 (NIV)

Here's the first thing: Jesus says **GO**, not come. He does not say we are to invite people to come and join us. We are to go to them. We must go where the people are.

Then notice he says **ALL**, not some. Make disciples of all, not just a few. The word 'nations' can also mean 'people groups', or even just 'people.' We might be tempted to pick and choose who we want to share God's good news with, trying to figure out who seems ready. But God said we need to share it with everyone, sow that seed — because we can never predict who will believe, who God could then use to go on and produce another bumper crop. Every disciple, every follower, has the potential to become a church. How?

Because they're **DISCIPLES**, not members of a club. Kai said that in his church they define a disciple as a learner who trains others. You can't call yourself a disciple until you train others to follow. Every disciple must learn from his teacher and become a trainer himself. It's not about sitting passively in church, waiting for self-help tips. It's about learning everything from Jesus and then telling everyone about Jesus. If each person tells just a few people who decide to follow, they in turn will tell more people, and the **✗ MULTIPLICATION** has started.

The 'training' process isn't complicated at all (remember Jesus' simple job interview at the beginning of this chapter?). Everyone can do this.

You just need to know **WHO**.

And then you need to know **HOW**.

The answer to **WHO** is "all the people around you." You can start by writing a list of people. I've noticed there are people everywhere! List people related to you or who you relate to at work. Put their names down and talk to God about them every day. Prayer, connecting with God, is the most important part. That's how God works with us and through us.

Next, the **HOW**. Write down your own unique story of how you got to know Jesus. Think it through, how you can share what God has done in your life. You don't need to wait to be a Bible expert, because you are the expert on your own life. "Listen to my story." You have your experience of life and how God has showed up in it. And every story that has Jesus in it is an adventure!

Finally introduce them to **JESUS' LOVE**. In everything you do and say, you need to be telling them, "God is sending me to tell you about his love. He wants to call you back home to him." Think of ways to show them what this love is like, by listening, being kind and generous — these are all ways the Bible would say you are blessing them.

When do you do this? Any time! Any chance, any place. It's part of the call: "Follow, and fish for people." We move from saying "yes" to doing "yes."

In this simple way, one Asian farmer managed to start 110 house churches in a year. In another town a 67-year-old woman became a Christian and in one year led more than 60 families to become believers. Every month, Kai's 'trainers' start two thousand house churches and small groups in villages, urban high-rise apartments and factories.

THE REASON THE CHURCH IN CHINA GROWS LIKE THIS IS THAT EVERYONE HAS THIS HEART - EVEN YOUNG CHILDREN AND VERY OLD PEOPLE, THEY KNOW THEY ARE CALLED, TO LEAD THE WHOLE OF THEIR FAMILY AND ALL THEIR FRIENDS TO KNOW CHRIST. IF NOT, HOW CAN YOU HAVE ANY PEACE YOURSELF? BECAUSE ONE DAY WHEN YOU MEET GOD, HE WILL ASK YOU, "WHERE IS HE? WHERE IS SHE? THAT PERSON FROM YOUR FAMILY? YOUR PARENTS? YOUR CHILDREN? YOUR RELATIVE? YOUR GOOD FRIEND? YOU HAD CHANCES TO SHARE THE GOOD NEWS WITH THEM, WHY DIDN'T YOU?"

Pastor Ying Kai

Now as I said, I'll pretty much do anything (I have pretty much done anything) to tell people about Jesus. When I went to Kenya to do a mission years ago, the church danced in the street. The young people spent the morning praying, then in the afternoon they just danced through the market place, and then people would join them, hold hands, come and sing and hear about Jesus. They just danced and worshipped God out in the street and had fun doing it. They always got new people coming along like that.

"I will celebrate before the Lord. I will become even more undignified than this, and I will be humiliated in my own eyes."

Declaration by David the king of Israel in 2 Samuel 6:21-22 (NIV)

There's something about being joyful that attracts people, isn't there?

So yes, I'd dance in the street, with my cheesy Christian t-shirt on, juggling and fire eating in front of strangers. Why not? So what if it's undignified? Someone might change their mind about God.

But look, I'll be honest. I said, "with strangers." Because I don't know about you, but it's at least a million times harder with people you know, than people you don't.

People who know you, I mean.

There was a time that Jesus healed a man, set him free from all kinds of hellish mental and spiritual torture. The guy just wanted to come and hang around Jesus, follow him like the other disciples. But Jesus instead told him to do the hard thing:

> *"Go home to your own people and tell them how much the Lord has done for you, and how he has had mercy on you." So the man went away and began to tell in the Decapolis how much Jesus had done for him. And all the people were amazed.*

Mark 5:19-20 (NIV)

Tell those close to you what God has done for you. About how he **LOVES** you and has a **PLAN** for your life, and **DREAMS** for you to **BELIEVE** in. How he wants to **BLESS** you and use you for **GREAT THINGS**.

Tell those close to you, what God has done for you. Your family: the toughest audience!

Because they say, "Who the heck are you these days? Get over yourself. When did you become captain of the God squad? God's got a plan and a dream for you, has he? God's spoken to you has he? Well that's great — but we know you. We know the real you."

The hardest to reach are closest to home.

You're in good company. Jesus himself knew exactly this kind of rejection from those closest to him. His own family didn't believe in him. They thought he was crazy. His brothers and sisters tried to take him away and divert him off course several times. It wasn't until after Jesus came back to life — beat death and proved that he really was who he said he was — that his own brother James came to the sudden realisation that his Big Bro was in fact the Big Guy. Only then did James make his way from brother to believer: to saying "My Lord and my God!"

How about our neighbours? Same story:

> *Jesus left there and went to his home town, accompanied by his disciples. When the Sabbath came, he began to teach in the synagogue, and many who heard him were amazed.*
>
> *"Where did this man get these things?" they asked. "What's this wisdom that has been given him? What are these remarkable miracles he is performing? Isn't this the carpenter? Isn't this Mary's son and the brother of James, Joseph, Judas and Simon? Aren't his sisters here with us?" And they took offence at him.*
>
> *Jesus said to them, "A prophet is not without honour except in his own town, among his relatives and in his own home."*

Mark 6:1-4 (NIV)

When Jesus tried to preach and teach and do miracles in his home town they didn't throw a party, they tried to throw him off a cliff.

So with people I don't know, I gladly do the fishing: bringing people (strangers, anyway) back to God. I'll chat with bus and taxi drivers, waiters, waitresses, people I meet when I'm walking the dog, people on trains: anywhere and everywhere.

But it's hard to talk to my brother about how Jesus loves him and wants to know him now and in heaven forever.

Because he's a City fan....

Not really. It's hard because he's "Our Terry!" We grew up together. Shared the same room until I was 16.

It's hard to talk to my Mum, my sister and Uncle Baz about Jesus. I love them all. But it's so much tougher because they have known me all my life. They know the old Anthony. How far away from God I once was.

And they also know that the new Anthony is not perfect by any stretch of the imagination.

Don't even get me started on the neighbours. They trimmed back the hedges in the garden without asking! I know Jesus said you're supposed to love your neighbours, but how on earth are you meant to forgive and forget something like that?

So what can we do?

Start with that first thing. Pray for them. Keep them in your conversations with God. Don't give up on them. God doesn't give up on us.

Jesus said, "Go and tell all people." It includes the toughest people to reach.

He doesn't mean just people in Mongolia or the Sudan. He means the person who shares your flat. The people you see at weddings and those other family occasions. The ones who work in your office. Who you've dismissed: "I'm sure they're never going to change their mind about God."

People like I used to be.

People like you used to be.

What changed?

Someone prayed. Someone cared. Someone shared.

Those words from Ying Kai burned me on the inside when I heard them: "One day you will stand before God and he will say, 'Where is your brother?'." God is going to ask me that question. Jesus once told a story where a man died and then begged for a chance to go and warn his brothers. But he was told it was too late then — there was no way back.

This one short life is our opportunity to be not merely members of a church, a club for people who said "yes" to Jesus, but to be disciples who are still learning, praying for all people, loving them, and sharing our story with them to help them find their way back to God, and to be saved for ∞ *INFINITY*.

Even if your neighbour or brother or friend shows no apparent interest in becoming a follower of Jesus, you don't know what God is doing in their lives, so don't ever give up. God loves everyone you will meet today, he is at work behind the scenes of their story for good. He's desperate for them to know his love. Everyone. Everywhere. And if you're his follower, you're qualified for the job! He will use anyone who believes in him, so if you're anyone, believe it.

WORKOUT

This **✗ MULTIPLICATION** starts with you! Make your list today. Write down the names. Don't leave off the toughest ones, put them at the top. **CONNECT** with God about them and pray every day for them.

1. _____

2. _____

3. _____

4. _____

5. _____

6. _____

7. _____

8. _____

9. _____

10. _____

Now think about your story. How has God worked in your life? What does he mean to you?

Write it down here:

_____

_____

_____

_____

_____

_____

_____

_____

_____

_____

_____

_____

_____

_____

_____

_____

_____

_____

_____

_____

_____

_____

_____

_____

_____

_____

_____

Take every opportunity to share it, and start seeing what God will do.

 **CONNECT**

Lord Jesus, you could write it across the sky but instead you've entrusted this message to me. You've got the authority to change the whole world, but you want me to play my part. You've made me Plan A, and there is no Plan B. So I will pray a dangerous, short prayer: **"USE ME."**

I want these people on my list to **WORK IT OUT** like I am trying to, to find their way back to God and to change their minds once and for **∞ INFINITY**.

Please help me live life with so much joy and hope no matter what, that my life raises the question to which you are the only possible answer -- and to share when they ask what you mean to me with anyone and everyone near or far who wants to know, so they can meet you too.

ADVANCE

"...you know you have a future in God."
1 Peter 1:21 (MSG)

So, where do you go from here? The answer is — just keep on **WORKING IT OUT**. You've reached the end of this book, looked at some of the lessons that God wanted to teach you. It's just the beginning! You won't ever master it all in this life, because there will always be new things God wants to show you about his character, and about who you are.

I ran a marathon a couple of years ago. But if I want to stay healthy I need to keep on flexing those muscles, pushing onwards. Otherwise it would be like I'd never been fit in the first place.

God describes what he does in our lives as like a heart transplant, but if you want to keep that new heart healthy, you need to trust God with your personal training. He's got a plan, perfectly suited to you: where you're at, right now.

> *Not that I have already obtained all this, or have already arrived at my goal, but I press on to take hold of that for which Christ Jesus took hold of me. Brothers and sisters, I do not consider myself yet to have taken hold of it. But one thing I do: forgetting what is behind and straining towards what is ahead, I press on towards the goal to win the prize for which God has called me heavenwards in Christ Jesus.*
>
> Philippians 3:12-14 (NIV)

So keep exploring: join all the other people who are **WORKING IT OUT**. Check out churches near you: some of them are good and some of them are awful, so look for one where they welcome new people who aren't perfect and you'll fit in. It's so much easier when you're not alone. You can read books, listen to podcasts, go on a course. Have a look at the list of suggestions over the page for inspiration. The good news gets better and better the more you find out and get to know God.

Who knows where you might end up?

"WITH GOD, NOTHING IS IMPOSSIBLE."

READ Get to know the Bible, a little bit at a time. There are notes and reading plans to guide you: why not start with *Word For Today*, which is produced by UCB. You can get a paper copy, a daily email or download the app onto your phone: **ucb.co.uk/word-for-today**

I've written a few books — *Rough Diamonds, The BEST Marriage, The (Don't Have) To Do List* and I have a blog, at **anthonydelaney.com**

GO Meet up with people who are also **WORKING IT OUT** and join a church. Or if you live in or near Manchester, why not come and join us at Ivy Church for one of our services. All the information is here: **ivychurch.org**

LISTEN You can listen to podcasts of the Ivy Church talks: **ivychurch.org**

LEARN The Alpha Course is a great way of exploring more about why Jesus came to live here on earth, who God is, and what it means to live our lives for him. There is almost certainly an Alpha Course at a church near you, maybe you've seen it advertised? Otherwise you can use their search tool to find one: **alpha.org/try**

Other courses are available! One great new one you could try looks at your own life story with its inevitable ups and downs and how God fits into that. Details at **mylifeworkshop.org**

WATCH . You could go to Ivy Church's YouTube channel **youtube.com/ivychurch** to watch some of the talks that we've put online.

WORD

"Your word is a lamp for my feet, a light on my path."

Psalm 119:105 (NIV)

Throughout this book you'll see lots of links to the Bible, and the messages that are written in it. People sometimes call the Bible 'The Word of God,' because they believe it's the best way of finding out what God thinks and does about things, even what he might be saying to you here and now.

It's not just one book, but a library of 66, covering everything from the beginning of time to true love and the end of life as we know it. Christians believe various people through time were inspired by God to write all the different parts. The more you get to know about the Bible, the more you find out about the God who is alive and working through it.

You'll find historical accounts, lessons, family trees, songs, warnings, letters, battle records, advice, predictions, poems, encouragements, speeches and dreams. The people in these books were experiencing war, famine, peace, pain, love, hope, temptation, riches, fear, kindness, surprises, threats, hate, happiness, depression, contentment and every other condition you could meet in the journey from life to death.

In other words, it was written by people like you, for people like you, but somehow God was speaking to and through them. People throughout history, coming up against the same sorts of challenges and experiences that anyone has ever had. And then God made himself part of it all, the Author climbing right into the heart of the Story.

If you have a copy of the Bible in book form, get it and open it up. You'll see on the index page that the two main sections are the Old Testament and the New Testament. Testament means 'Promise.' Promise One is the story leading up to Jesus being born, and the next is of God's Promise fulfilled, from Jesus' birth onwards. These sections are divided into books, written by different authors, at different points in time.

Here they are:

THE OLD TESTAMENT

Genesis
Exodus
Leviticus
Numbers
Deuteronomy
Joshua
Judges
Ruth
1 Samuel
2 Samuel
1 Kings
2 Kings
1 Chronicles
2 Chronicles
Ezra
Nehemiah
Esther
Job

The first few books of the Bible tell the stories of the earliest people on earth, and how their families grew into our nations. People find themselves getting into a mess, and God has to keep pointing out the boundaries. Rules for a healthy and moral life.

Psalms
Proverbs
Ecclesiastes
Song of Solomon

God inspires poets and songwriters to compose messages about how much he loves his people, as he comes back time after time to pick them up out of the dirt and destruction they keep getting into.

Isaiah
Jeremiah
Lamentations
Ezekiel
Daniel
Hosea
Joel
Amos
Obadiah
Jonah

Eventually God speaks to prophets, people who can give encouragement, warnings and predictions about what's going to happen in the future. It's all looking a bit bleak at times but with lots of hints of a bright hope to come.

Micah
Nahum
Habakkuk
Zephaniah
Haggai
Zechariah
Malachi

Then it goes quiet. Waiting on the Promise.

THE NEW TESTAMENT

Matthew
Mark
Luke
John

Two thirds through the Bible, we reach the hinge of history. A tiny baby is born, and God's radical message of love takes on a new relevance. Four books (called the Gospels, or 'good news') cover the events of Jesus' life on earth, as eye witnesses give their first hand accounts. Not everything Jesus did, but what they felt was most important to help us believe.

Acts

The next book begins to recount the dramatic lives of Jesus' followers after he went back to heaven. This book doesn't end because every day now we get to add to it!

Romans
1 Corinthians
2 Corinthians
Galatians
Ephesians
Philippians
Colossians
1 Thessalonians
2 Thessalonians
1 Timothy

There are letters from some of the key characters of those times to all the new believers, with teaching and encouragement to live changed lives in community together.

2 Timothy
Titus
Philemon
Hebrews
James
1 Peter
2 Peter
1 John
2 John
3 John
Jude

Revelation

Finally, a vision of the future, with spectacular descriptions of how things will be as this earth ends.

 ## NAVIGATE

When I first started to read the Bible, I thought the references to locations looked a bit cryptic — they can if you're not used to it. But it's not actually any harder to work out than an address or link to a web page. You need to know where you're going to, and this gives you directions to the right place.

All the books in the Bible are divided into chapters, and then each chapter into verses. So you can go immediately to the exact point that you need to, just by using this key.

Here's how it works. I can give you the reference *John 3:16 (NIV)*, so first you would check out the page number of the book called 'John' in the index. You can see this book is listed in the New Testament (John was one of Jesus' friends, he wrote one of the four life accounts).

3 is the Chapter number, so flick through the chapters until you get to the third one (it will be labelled).

Then work your way down the text until you get to the 16th verse — your destination. All the chapters and books are printed at the top of each page, so you always know exactly where you are.

"For God so loved the world that he gave his one and only son, that whoever believes in him shall not perish but have eternal life."
John 3:16 (NIV)

The last section in brackets is the translation that I'm using. As it was put together over thousands of years by many authors in different areas of the world, the Bible was not originally written in just one language. Most of the Old Testament was in Hebrew, the New Testament was written in Greek, and there are also some portions written in Aramaic. None of it was in English — the first English translations of the Bible were published about 500 years ago. Since then it has been modernised and carefully translated by historians, linguists and scholars so that we can understand it clearly in our society today.

There are many English language versions available: you can check them out online. Of course, the main message of each sentence is the same in any translation, and this doesn't change — you can always locate the verse or story that you need to by navigating like we did just now. You might find that one particular version works best for you — you can make up your mind on this as you start to **WORK IT OUT**.